Bitcoin Essentials

Gain insights into Bitcoin, a cryptocurrency and
a powerful technology, to optimize your Bitcoin
mining techniques

Albert Szmigielski

[PACKT] open source *
PUBLISHING   community experience distilled

BIRMINGHAM - MUMBAI

Bitcoin Essentials

First published: February 2016

Production reference: 1170216

Published by Packt Publishing Ltd.
Livery Place
35 Livery Street
Birmingham B3 2PB, UK.

ISBN 978-1-78528-197-6

www.packtpub.com

Credits

Author
Albert Szmigielski

Reviewer
Kevin M. Fitzgerald

Commissioning Editor
Edward Bowkett

Acquisition Editor
Ruchita Bhansali

Content Development Editor
Sanjeet Rao

Technical Editor
Saurabh Malhotra

Copy Editor
Sneha Singh

Project Coordinator
Judie Jose

Proofreader
Safis Editing

Indexer
Priya Sane

Production Coordinator
Shantanu N. Zagade

Cover Work
Shantanu N. Zagade

About the Author

Albert Szmigielski is a thinker, a computing scientist, a software engineer, and a blockchain professional. He holds a BSc in Computer Science and an MSc in Digital Currency. He has been involved in a number of start-ups and software projects. He believes in a decentralized, distributed nature of storing information, and hence has an interest in Bitcoin and blockchain technology.

Albert is a researcher at CryptoIQ and a mentor at the Blockchain Institute. He frequently contributes to his blog at `blog.cryptoIQ.ca`.

I would like to thank Carla Miller for her support and general feedback. I would also like to thank my family; they give meaning to my life.

About the Reviewer

Kevin M. Fitzgerald is the platform architect for Okanjo.com. He has well over a decade of development experience in education, medical systems, and start-ups. He has been tinkering with the Web since dial-up modems went mainstream.

He is active in the Open Source community and has contributed to the Mono project and also to Umbraco communities. He continues to be active on GitHub, working with the latest technologies and projects. He has also contributed to the book *WebGL Game Development* by Sumeet Arora.

He and his wife, Luciana, are celebrating their seventh year of marriage and enjoy long walks on the beach with their daughter, Rosalia, talking about Node.js, C#, and Bitcoin.

www.PacktPub.com

eBooks, discount offers, and more

Did you know that Packt offers eBook versions of every book published, with PDF and ePub files available? You can upgrade to the eBook version at www.PacktPub.com and as a print book customer, you are entitled to a discount on the eBook copy. Get in touch with us at customercare@packtpub.com for more details.

At www.PacktPub.com, you can also read a collection of free technical articles, sign up for a range of free newsletters and receive exclusive discounts and offers on Packt books and eBooks.

https://www2.packtpub.com/books/subscription/packtlib

Do you need instant solutions to your IT questions? PacktLib is Packt's online digital book library. Here, you can search, access, and read Packt's entire library of books.

Why subscribe?

- Fully searchable across every book published by Packt
- Copy and paste, print, and bookmark content
- On demand and accessible via a web browser

Table of Contents

Preface   **v**

Chapter 1: Bitcoin Wallets and Mining Software   **1**

  Bitcoin wallets   **1**

    What is a Bitcoin wallet?   2

    Why do we need Bitcoin wallets?   2

  Types of wallets   **3**

    Software wallets   3

    Hardware wallets   12

    Full wallet versus thin client   13

    Hosted wallets   13

    Wallet security   14

  Mining software   **14**

    The need for mining software   14

    What does mining software do?   15

    Which mining software to choose?   15

  Summary   **23**

Chapter 2: CPU Mining   **25**

  Mining with Bitcoin Core   **25**

    Mining software   29

    Let's start mining   31

  Pros and cons of mining   **32**

    Pros of mining   32

    Cons of mining   32

  Best practices when mining with CPUs   **33**

  Profitability of mining   **34**

  Summary   **35**

Chapter 3: GPU Mining	**37**
Setting up a GPU for mining	**37**
Drivers	38
Mining software	39
Windows installation instructions	40
Linux installation instructions	40
Let's start mining	42
Multiple GPU setup	44
Mining on a GPU	45
Pros and cons of GPU mining	**46**
Pros of GPU mining	46
Cons of GPU mining	46
Best practices when mining with GPUs	**47**
Benchmarks of mining speeds with different GPUs	**48**
GPU versus CPU mining	**49**
Profitability of GPU mining	**49**
Summary	**50**
Chapter 4: FPGA Mining	**51**
Setup and installation of the required software	**51**
Mining software	52
Linux installation instructions	52
Windows installation instructions	53
Let's start mining	54
What happens when mining on a FPGA	55
Pros and cons of FPGA mining	**55**
Pros of FPGA mining	55
Cons of FPGA mining	56
Best practices when mining with FPGAs	**56**
Benchmarks of mining speeds with different FPGAs	**57**
FPGA versus GPU and CPU mining	**57**
Profitability of FPGA mining	**58**
Summary	**59**
Chapter 5: ASIC Mining	**61**
Setting up mining software	**62**
Drivers	62
Mining software	62
Installing cgminer on Linux	62
Installing cgminer on Windows	64
Let's start mining	67
What happens when mining on a ASIC	69

Pros and cons of ASIC mining   **70**
  Pros of ASIC mining   70
  Cons of ASIC mining   70
Best practices when mining with ASICs   **71**
Benchmarks of mining speeds with different ASICs   **72**
ASIC versus FPGA, GPU, and CPU mining   **73**
Profitability of ASIC mining   **73**
Summary   **74**
Chapter 6: Solo Versus Pool Mining   **75**
Solo mining   **75**
  Setting up a wallet for solo mining   76
  Setting up mining software for solo mining   78
  Setting up mining software for pool mining   79
Pool mining discussion   **82**
  Mining pools   83
  Choosing a pool   84
  Solo versus pool mining   85
  Profitability   85
Majority attack on Bitcoin   **85**
  51% attack   86
Summary   **86**
Chapter 7: Large Scale Mining   **87**
Large Scale Mining overview   **87**
Large Scale Mining challenges   **90**
  Inexpensive and reliable electricity   90
  Good network connectivity   90
  Access to latest hardware   90
  Stable political climate   91
  Bitcoin exchange rate   91
  Cooling of mining hardware   91
Large Scale Mining operations   **92**
  BitFury   94
  KnC Miner   94
  21 INC   95
  Mega Big Power   95
  Genesis Mining   96
  Other mine operators   96
Summary   **97**

Chapter 8: The Future of Bitcoin Mining   99
Overview of the current state of mining   99
Further centralization of mining   100
Hardware arms race   100
Halving of the reward   100
Consolidation, mergers, and acquisitions   101
Bitcoin exchange rate   101
Quantum computing and mining   101
Cracking the security of SHA-256   101
Centralization by region   102
Governments adopting cryptocurrencies   102
Decentralization of mining   102
Mining chips everywhere   103
21 INC and the Bitcoin Computer   103
Mining devices as a source of heat   103
The end of the ASIC arms race is near   103
Decentralized mining is key   104
Elimination of PoW   104
Inefficiency of PoW   104
Replacement of PoW   104
Can we do without mining?   105
Replacing or eliminating mining   105
Efficiency of mining   106
Possible ways that mining may change   106
Summary   107
Index   109

Preface

Surely, by now you have heard of the phenomenon called Bitcoin. Is it digital money, is it a payment system, is it a network, or is it something else? The answer is yes to all the previous questions. Bitcoin is all of those and more. In this book, we will concentrate on the mining aspect of Bitcoin. Mining is how new bitcoins are created and how transactions are accepted into the Bitcoin blockchain. We will show you how to mine for yourself, if you are interested. We explain step-by-step what is necessary and how to do it. CPU, GPU, FPGA, and ASIC mining is also discussed. We will examine solo mining and pool mining. We will spend a little bit of time taking a look at large mining operations. Finally, we will speculate what the future may look like in the mining world of Bitcoin.

What this book covers

Chapter 1, *Bitcoin Wallets and Mining Software*, gives an overview of Bitcoin wallets: hardware, software, full and thin clients. The chapter also discusses mining software.

Chapter 2, *CPU Mining*, looks at Bitcoin mining using a CPU. It covers everything you need to get started.

Chapter 3, *GPU Mining*, concentrates on GPU mining. It covers GPU driver setup, mining software setup, and it touches upon practical mining issues. Examples are included.

Chapter 4, *FPGA Mining*, examines FPGA mining, including software, drivers, and a discussion of best practices.

Chapter 5, *ASIC Mining*, looks at ASIC mining in detail. We set up the software that is needed to mine and we show you practical examples of mining with ASICS.

Chapter 6, *Solo Versus Pool Mining*, explains solo and pool mining and weighs the pros and cons of both ways of mining.

Chapter 7, Large Scale Mining, looks at mining as a business. There are a handful companies that decided to mine for profit. They represent the bleeding edge in mining techniques.

Chapter 8, The Future of Bitcoin Mining, speculates how mining may evolve in the future. We look at the possibility of mining becoming more centralized and the possibility of mining becoming decentralized.

What you need for this book

You will need a computer, preferably running Linux, but Windows and OS X is fine as well. You will also need an internet connection. If you'd like to try mining with a GPU, FPGA, or ASIC, you would need to have one (or more) of those hardware pieces. All software is open source and can be downloaded from the internet. We provide links in the chapters to the required software.

Who this book is for

If you have never mined before, this book will ensure that you know what mining is all about. If you are familiar with Bitcoin mining, then it will help you to optimize your mining operations at a deeper level. A basic understanding of computers and operating systems is assumed and some familiarity with cryptocurrency basics would be an added advantage.

Conventions

In this book, you will find a number of text styles that distinguish between different kinds of information. Here are some examples of these styles and an explanation of their meaning.

Code words in text, database table names, folder names, filenames, file extensions, pathnames, dummy URLs, user input, and Twitter handles are shown as follows: "Execute the `getmininginfo` command in the console of the Bitcoin Core wallet."

Any command-line input or output is written as follows:

```
./minerd --url <poolurl:port> --userpass <USERNAME.WORKER:PASSWORD>
-a<algorithm>
```

New terms and important words are shown in bold. Words that you see on the screen, for example, in menus or dialog boxes, appear in the text like this: "Now click on the **Help** menu and select **Debug Window**."

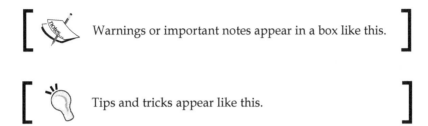

Warnings or important notes appear in a box like this.

Tips and tricks appear like this.

Reader feedback

Feedback from our readers is always welcome. Let us know what you think about this book — what you liked or disliked. Reader feedback is important for us as it helps us develop titles that you will really get the most out of.

To send us general feedback, simply e-mail feedback@packtpub.com, and mention the book's title in the subject of your message.

If there is a topic that you have expertise in and you are interested in either writing or contributing to a book, see our author guide at www.packtpub.com/authors.

Customer support

Now that you are the proud owner of a Packt book, we have a number of things to help you to get the most from your purchase.

Downloading the color images of this book

We also provide you with a PDF file that has color images of the screenshots/ diagrams used in this book. The color images will help you better understand the changes in the output. You can download this file from http://www.packtpub.com/ sites/default/files/downloads/BitcoinEssentials_ColorImages.pdf.

Errata

Although we have taken every care to ensure the accuracy of our content, mistakes do happen. If you find a mistake in one of our books—maybe a mistake in the text or the code—we would be grateful if you could report this to us. By doing so, you can save other readers from frustration and help us improve subsequent versions of this book. If you find any errata, please report them by visiting http://www.packtpub.com/submit-errata, selecting your book, clicking on the **Errata Submission Form** link, and entering the details of your errata. Once your errata are verified, your submission will be accepted and the errata will be uploaded to our website or added to any list of existing errata under the Errata section of that title.

To view the previously submitted errata, go to https://www.packtpub.com/books/content/support and enter the name of the book in the search field. The required information will appear under the **Errata** section.

Piracy

Piracy of copyrighted material on the Internet is an ongoing problem across all media. At Packt, we take the protection of our copyright and licenses very seriously. If you come across any illegal copies of our works in any form on the Internet, please provide us with the location address or website name immediately so that we can pursue a remedy.

Please contact us at copyright@packtpub.com with a link to the suspected pirated material.

We appreciate your help in protecting our authors and our ability to bring you valuable content.

Questions

If you have a problem with any aspect of this book, you can contact us at questions@packtpub.com, and we will do our best to address the problem.

1
Bitcoin Wallets and Mining Software

In this chapter, we will take a look at the various Bitcoin wallets available, explore the mining software that is currently available, review the functions that Bitcoin wallets perform, and why we need them. We will take a brief look at both software and hardware wallets. The difference between full wallets and thin client wallets will also be explored. We will also touch upon hosted wallets and look into wallet security.

Next, we will take a brief look at mining software and examine why the software is needed and what it does. Finally, we will quickly review what mining software is available to us and which software we should use. Keep in mind that the material presented in this chapter will be brief and serve only as a review of the basics:

- Bitcoin wallets
- Types of wallets
- Wallet security
- Mining software

Bitcoin wallets

In this section, we will take a closer look at Bitcoin wallets. We will define what a wallet is and explain why we need a wallet. We will look at the types of wallets available. There are software and hardware wallets, full wallets, and the so-called thin wallets. There are also hosted wallets that are run by companies for the users' convenience. We will look at the most popular wallet called **Bitcoin Core**; finally, we will touch upon wallet security.

What is a Bitcoin wallet?

A Bitcoin wallet (sometimes called a client) is a software that facilitates performing bitcoin transactions. Wallets come in different flavors. The most capable of them are called **full clients**. They can perform bitcoin transactions and act as a gateway to the Bitcoin network. Full clients also store a copy of the Bitcoin block chain locally. An example of a full client is the Bitcoin Core software application.

Definition

Block chain: The Bitcoin database that stores all the transaction data is called a block chain. The transactions are grouped together in batches for efficiency reasons. A batch is called a block and each block (except for the first, called genesis block) has a link to the previous block. This linking together of blocks is the chain part of the block chain.

A wallet allows us to send (spend) and receive bitcoins. These are the main transactions that most users will perform. Most importantly, a wallet stores your secret private keys, so that you can access the bitcoins you own. The name "wallet" is slightly misleading. The wallet actually does not store bitcoins directly. All the bitcoins are stored on the block chain and the wallet software simply allows you to transact with the bitcoins that the private keys stored in the wallet have control over. In simpler terms, wallets store private keys. Those keys are tied to bitcoins on the block chain and therefore you can send them to another address.

A wallet also allows us to look into the Bitcoin network and see additional details. It allows us to see information about the Bitcoin network, the block chain, mining, and the wallet in general. We will go over these in later chapters.

Why do we need Bitcoin wallets?

As mentioned earlier, wallets facilitate Bitcoin transactions. Without them, moving bitcoins from one address to another would be impossible. It is worth noting that a wallet is a fundamental piece of Bitcoin software. A wallet is the required software in order for the Bitcoin network to exist.

Without the ability to transfer bitcoins, the system would not be very useful. In the original wallet called **bitcoind**, the transactions had to be put together *manually*. Later on, the wallet software was expanded and updated to make transaction creation seem like a breeze. Since wallets connect us to the Bitcoin network, they are also needed in mining operations. While mining, it is the wallet software that communicates with the Bitcoin network. It watches out for new blocks, so that if a new block is found by some other participant, our mining software can stop working on the now *solved* block and move on to the next.

The transactions that our mining software will put in a candidate block also come from the wallet. In addition, wallets verify found blocks and propagate transactions that come onto the network.

Types of wallets

Wallets have come a long way since the original came out in 2009. There are now software wallets, hardware wallets, paper wallets, hosted wallets, and, of course, there are innovative companies who constantly think up new ways to create wallets.

Software wallets

There are a variety of software wallets. For an up-to-date list of the most popular wallets, see `https://bitcoin.org/en/choose-your-wallet`. We will concentrate here on the Bitcoin Core software application. At the time of writing this book, the current version is 0.11.2. You can always check the latest version here: `https://bitcoin.org/en/download`.

If you do not have Bitcoin Core installed and you would like to mine solo (solo mining will be explained in *Chapter 6, Solo Versus Pool Mining*), it would be a good idea to download and install it. Make sure that you have sufficient space on your hard drive for the block chain, which currently (Feb 2016) is about 55 GB. Once you install Bitcoin Core, it will proceed to download the block chain, which may take a while. When you open the software, you will be greeted with the following screen:

Fig. 1.1: The Bitcoin Core wallet.

As you can see, the client is downloading the block chain by synchronizing with the Bitcoin network. There are tabs to send and receive bitcoins. There is also a **Transactions** tab, under which you can find a history of all transactions performed with the wallet.

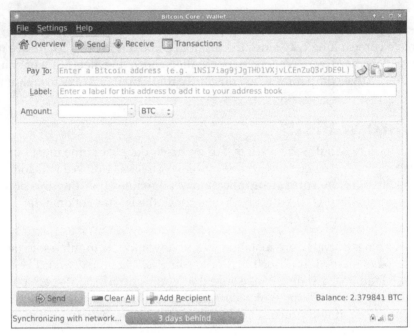

Fig. 1.2: Send tab in the Bitcoin Core wallet.

The **Send** tab can be used to transfer the bitcoins you control to another address. It requires a destination Bitcoin address and the amount you wish to transfer. If your wallet is password-protected (more on securing your wallet later), you will be prompted to enter it.

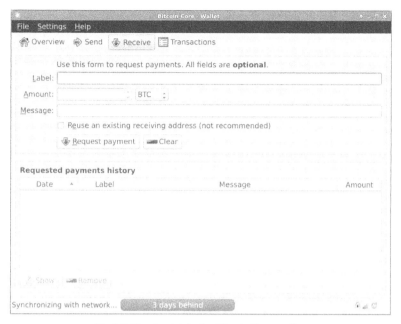

Fig. 1.3: Receive tab in the Bitcoin Core wallet.

The **Receive** screen, on entering the relevant information and pressing **Request payment**, will generate a QR code and a URI that can be sent out or posted online.

Fig. 1.4: Request payment screen, generated by Bitcoin Core

The **Transactions** tab lists all the transactions tied to the private keys that the wallet is storing.

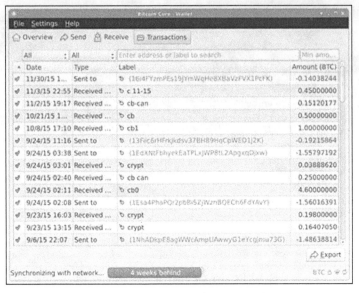

Fig. 1.5: The Transactions tab in Bitcoin Core

The functions described in the preceding section are the basic wallet transaction types, but what is more interesting is the information we can get about the network through the Bitcoin console. The console can be accessed by going to the **Help** menu and selecting **Debug window**.

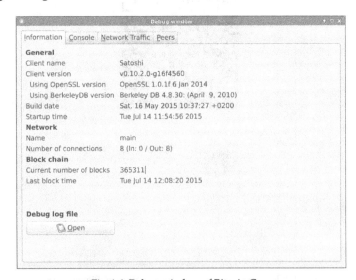

Fig. 1.6: Debug window of Bitcoin Core

Select the **Console** tab and you will be able to obtain a trove of information about the Bitcoin network and about Bitcoin's block chain. To see a list of possible commands, type `help` into the console and press *Enter*. You will be presented with a long list of commands that have been grouped in categories. A complete overview of the commands is beyond the scope of this book. However, we will take a look at some of them.

```
                        Debug window                      ↑ _ □ X
```

Information Console Network Traffic Peers

```
ping

== Rawtransactions ==
createrawtransaction [{"txid":"id","vout":n},...] {"address":amount,...}
decoderawtransaction "hexstring"
decodescript "hex"
getrawtransaction "txid" ( verbose )
sendrawtransaction "hexstring" ( allowhighfees )
signrawtransaction "hexstring" (
[{"txid":"id","vout":n,"scriptPubKey":"hex","redeemScript":"hex"},...]
["privatekey1",...] sighashtype )

== Util ==
createmultisig nrequired ["key",...]
estimatefee nblocks
estimatepriority nblocks
validateaddress "bitcoinaddress"
verifymessage "bitcoinaddress" "signature" "message"

== Wallet ==
addmultisigaddress nrequired ["key",...] ( "account" )
backupwallet "destination"
dumpprivkey "bitcoinaddress"
dumpwallet "filename"
getaccount "bitcoinaddress"
getaccountaddress "account"
getaddressesbyaccount "account"
getbalance ( "account" minconf includeWatchonly )
getnewaddress ( "account" )
getrawchangeaddress
getreceivedbyaccount "account" ( minconf )
getreceivedbyaddress "bitcoinaddress" ( minconf )
gettransaction "txid" ( includeWatchonly )
getunconfirmedbalance
getwalletinfo
importaddress "address" ( "label" rescan )
importprivkey "bitcoinprivkey" ( "label" rescan )
importwallet "filename"
keypoolrefill ( newsize )
listaccounts ( minconf includeWatchonly)
listaddressgroupings
listlockunspent
listreceivedbyaccount ( minconf includeempty includeWatchonly)
listreceivedbyaddress ( minconf includeempty includeWatchonly)
```

>

Fig. 1.7: A listing of all available commands

Perhaps, the most interesting to us will be the `getmininginfo` command. Typing it into the console yields the following:

```
                                   Debug window                              ↑ ▢ ✕

  Information  Console  Network Traffic  Peers

        listreceivedbyaddress ( minconf includeempty includeWatchonly)
        listsinceblock ( "blockhash" target-confirmations includeWatchonly)
        listtransactions ( "account" count from includeWatchonly)
        listunspent ( minconf maxconf ["address",...] )
        lockunspent unlock [{"txid":"txid","vout":n},...]
        move "fromaccount" "toaccount" amount ( minconf "comment" )
        sendfrom "fromaccount" "tobitcoinaddress" amount ( minconf "comment" "comment-to" )
        sendmany "fromaccount" {"address":amount,...} ( minconf "comment" )
        sendtoaddress "bitcoinaddress" amount ( "comment" "comment-to" )
        setaccount "bitcoinaddress" "account"
        settxfee amount
        signmessage "bitcoinaddress" "message"
        walletlock
        walletpassphrase "passphrase" timeout
        walletpassphrasechange "oldpassphrase" "newpassphrase"
  11:19:38   getmininginfo
  11:19:38   {
        "blocks" : 365306,
        "currentblocksize" : 0,
        "currentblocktx" : 0,
        "difficulty" : 51076366303.48192596,
        "errors" : "",
        "genproclimit" : -1,
        "networkhashps" : 353872920536823808,
        "pooledtx" : 44,
        "testnet" : false,
        "chain" : "main",
        "generate" : false,
        "hashespersec" : 0
        }

  >
```

Fig. 1.8: The getmininginfo command

As we can see, the command returns the last block number, current mining difficulty, network hashing speed, and some other information as well. There are websites that check this information for each block and offer graphs to visualize the data. They are called block explorers and there are many of them. The most popular perhaps is `http://blockchain.info`.

You can find out more information about any command by typing `help` followed by the command name. For example, to find out more about the `getmininginfo` command, we will type `help getmininginfo`:

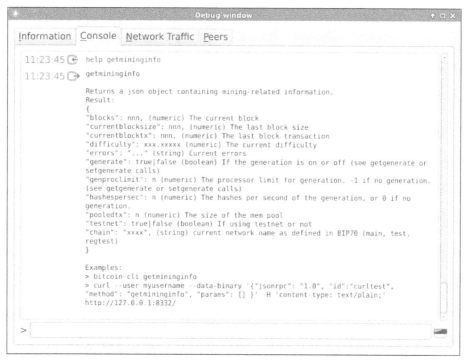

Fig. 1.9: Getting more information about a command: help getmininginfo

Another interesting command from a mining point of view is the `getblockchaininfo` command. The following screenshot shows us the output and the help data on that command:

```
                            Debug window                          ↑ □ ✕

 Information  Console  Network Traffic  Peers

 11:23:11 ⇐  getblockchaininfo

 11:23:11 ⇒  {
              "chain" : "main",
              "blocks" : 365307,
              "headers" : 365307,
              "bestblockhash" :
              "00000000000000000eecb8c5dabfede194627d53fddfdb685103e5317a7e175e",
              "difficulty" : 51076366303.48192596,
              "verificationprogress" : 0.99999694,
              "chainwork" : "000000000000000000000000000000000000000000086c2a008be061f61af648"
             }

 11:23:29 ⇐  help getblockchaininfo

 11:23:29 ⇒  getblockchaininfo
              Returns an object containing various state info regarding block chain processing.

              Result:
              {
              "chain": "xxxx", (string) current network name as defined in BIP70 (main, test,
              regtest)
              "blocks": xxxxxx, (numeric) the current number of blocks processed in the server
              "headers": xxxxxx, (numeric) the current number of headers we have validated
              "bestblockhash": "...", (string) the hash of the currently best block
              "difficulty": xxxxxx, (numeric) the current difficulty
              "verificationprogress": xxxx, (numeric) estimate of verification progress [0..1]
              "chainwork": "xxxx" (string) total amount of work in active chain, in hexadecimal
              }

              Examples:
              > bitcoin-cli getblockchaininfo
              > curl --user myusername --data-binary '{"jsonrpc": "1.0", "id":"curltest",
              "method": "getblockchaininfo", "params": [] }' -H 'content-type: text/plain;'
              http://127.0.0.1:8332/

 >
```

Fig. 1.10: Output of the getblockchain info command and help getblockchain info

Hardware wallets

Hardware wallets are a relatively new addition to the array of Bitcoin wallets available. They are not required for mining purposes, but are great for keeping your bitcoins safe. The two most popular solutions on the market are Trezor and Ledger wallets. We encourage you to take a look at their respective websites, if you think you can benefit from a hardware wallet.

Outside resources

Trezor website: `https://www.bitcointrezor.com/`

Ledger website: `https://www.ledgerwallet.com/`

The major advantage of hardware wallets over software ones is their security. They are not affected by computer viruses designed to attack software wallets. They are offline for a majority of the time (online only to compose a transaction). They also enjoy an advantage over paper wallets, as a result of being interactive versus importing the whole wallet, as in the case of a paper wallet.

Full wallet versus thin client

Any wallet that stores the entire block chain database is regarded as a full wallet, Bitcoin Core is one example. Sometimes there just aren't enough resources available to download and store the complete block chain. This could be due to bandwidth restrictions, storage limitations, or perhaps just an unwillingness to run the full wallet.

There are wallets available that do not download the entire block chain. This is obviously required for mobile computers with limited storage, such as smart phones and tablets and other Internet-of-things devices. These types of wallets are called thin clients. They use a procedure called **Simplified Payment Verification** (**SPV**) to avoid having a full copy of the block chain. SPV is not important for mining purposes, but every miner should at least know that the security of an SPV wallet is not as tight as the security of a full wallet.

Hosted wallets

There are a number of companies that offer hosted wallet services. This means that you do not need to download or install any software and of course downloading the block chain is also not required. There is a trade-off when you use a hosted wallet. You are giving away a part of the security that comes with running your own wallet in exchange for convenience.

However, as these hosted wallet companies are maturing and becoming big, their ways of securing bitcoins may be better than that of a single user. The risk of insolvency is then the biggest risk to a hosted wallet user. If the company goes bankrupt, then the funds stored in their hosted wallets will most likely not be recoverable. Just like with a traditional bank, deposits are liabilities of the bank and in the case of failure, depositors would only be able to recover the portion of their deposits that is insured by the government. We are not aware of any such insurance schemes available to hosted wallet providers.

Wallet security

Securing your wallet is a serious matter. With Bitcoin being deflationary, the value of the cryptocurrency is expected to rise in the long term. Therefore, making sure that your funds are only accessible to you is a worthwhile undertaking. Your online wallet should be encrypted and password-protected. Furthermore, you should back-up your password protected wallet to multiple locations.

To encrypt your wallet, select **Encrypt Wallet** from the **Settings** menu in Bitcoin Core and then follow the rest of the instructions. Please remember to choose a very strong password.

Make sure to use upper- and lower-case characters; also add some special characters and make the password long (min. 10 characters). It is also possible to make a passphrase out of ten (or more) random words. It will be beneficial if those words are not in a dictionary (use misspellings or combination words).

Finally, it is a good idea to only keep a small amount of bitcoins in your online wallet. The bulk of your holdings should be kept offline. A full discussion of securing your wallet is impossible here. We do encourage you to find resources online to educate yourself more about this topic.

Mining software

Let's now look at mining software. At the very beginning, mining software was built into the wallet software. Mining used only a single core of a CPU back then. Nowadays, there are a variety of devices that can perform the mining function. As such, there is some software needed to coordinate and manage the work done by these devices.

The need for mining software

As mentioned earlier, mining software coordinates and manages the work of different mining devices. In order for mining to move beyond utilizing a single core of a CPU, software was needed that could manage the work that multiple cores perform. This is to make sure that they do not do redundant work; hence, mining software was born. Later on, mining moved onto a multitude of devices and the need for a management software became even more apparent.

What does mining software do?

Bitcoin mining is basically a guessing game. The software constructs a candidate block. A candidate block includes the hash of the previous (last) block and it also includes transactions taken from the pending transaction pool. Finally, it includes the most important piece, called a nonce. A nonce is basically a counter. The software constructs the candidate block and then hashes it. If the result does not meet the difficulty criteria, then the nonce is incremented and another hash is taken.

Mining devices can make billions and even trillions of these hashes per second. When a successful hash is found, the software submits the solved block to the network for verification. We call this guessing rather than solving because solving implies a method other than repeated guessing and checking if it is correct.

Which mining software to choose?

There are a variety of different software miners. A good comprehensive list can be found at: `https://en.bitcoin.it/wiki/Mining_software`. The two most popular miners are cgminer and bfgminer; both are open source and can be downloaded from GitHub. Here, we will concentrate on cgminer.

Cgminer can be downloaded from a variety of sources on the Internet. We recommend going directly to the developer's website: `http://ck.kolivas.org/apps/cgminer/`.

Cgminer is available for Windows and Linux systems and it can also be built from source for Mac OS; there are also third party providers that host a compiled Mac OS version on their websites. Download the appropriate version for your system. Installation on Windows systems is straightforward. As an example, we are going to use cgminer version 3.7.2. This is the last version to support GPU mining; keep this in mind if you want to mine with your GPUs. (We will further discuss the versions of cgminer in the chapters on mining with specific devices.)

Defintion
GPU: Graphics Processing Unit is a processor designed specifically for processing and displaying graphics on a computer screen.

Once you have cgminer installed, you may want to verify it by running the `cgminer -n` command in your terminal (also called command prompt in Windows). The output will look similar to this:

```
Command Prompt                                    _  □  ×

C:\CRYPTO\cgminer-3.7.2-windows>
C:\CRYPTO\cgminer-3.7.2-windows>
C:\CRYPTO\cgminer-3.7.2-windows>cgminer -n
 [2015-07-22 13:54:45] CL Platform 0 vendor: Advanced Micro Devices, Inc.

 [2015-07-22 13:54:45] CL Platform 0 name: AMD Accelerated Parallel Processing

 [2015-07-22 13:54:45] CL Platform 0 version: OpenCL 1.2 AMD-APP (1348.5)

 [2015-07-22 13:54:45] Platform 0 devices: 1
 [2015-07-22 13:54:45]  0         Pitcairn
 [2015-07-22 13:54:45] GPU 0 AMD Radeon R9 200 Series hardware monitoring enable
d
 [2015-07-22 13:54:45] 1 GPU devices max detected
 [2015-07-22 13:54:45] USB all: found 11 devices - listing known devices

 [2015-07-22 13:54:45] No known USB devices

C:\CRYPTO\cgminer-3.7.2-windows>_
```

Fig. 1.11: Output from the cgminer -n command

It lists the required software (OpenCL in our case) and confirms that cgminer found some hardware in your system that it can use to mine. In our case, it is an AMD R9 Radeon GPU.

Now would be a good time to start cgminer and familiarize ourselves with the basic features. In order to run cgminer, we need to tell it where to get work from. This means a mining pool or your local wallet if you are mining solo (more on this will follow in the chapters on mining solo or with a pool).

Definition

Mining pool: Bitcoin mining is very competitive and in order to have a better chance at being successful, individual miners combine their resources together and form groups, also called pools. Such a combined mining group is called a mining pool. A quick Internet search will show that there are a number of mining pools out there.

If you are already registered with a pool, run the following command to start mining:

`cgminer -o <http://pool:port> -u <username> -p <password>`

This tells cgminer to connect to the specified pool with the specified credentials (of course, replace the values in the angle brackets with your own pool information).

If successful, cgminer will start and display the following screen:

```
Command Prompt - cgminer -c C:\CRYPTO\cgminer-config\cgminer-multi...  —  ☐  ×
cgminer version 3.7.2 - Started: [2015-07-22 13:23:30]
---------------------------------------------------------------------------
(15s):136.7M (avg):350.4Mh/s | A:0  R:0  HW:0  WU:3.9/m
ST: 2  SS: 0  NB: 1  LW: 6  GF: 0  RF: 0
Connected to us-west.multipool.us diff 256 with stratum as user 0xfffff.280x
Block: 1d4d1f7d...  Diff:1.9K  Started: [13:23:30]  Best share: 2
---------------------------------------------------------------------------
[P]ool management [G]PU management [S]ettings [D]isplay options [Q]uit
GPU 0:  52.0C 1151RPM | 212.8M/613.2Mh/s | A:0 R:0 HW:0 WU: 7.8/m I:13
---------------------------------------------------------------------------

[2015-07-22 13:23:26] Started cgminer 3.7.2
[2015-07-22 13:23:26] Loaded configuration file C:\CRYPTO\cgminer-config\cgmine
r-multipool-sha256-q6600.conf
[2015-07-22 13:23:29] Probing for an alive pool
[2015-07-22 13:23:29] Pool 0 difficulty changed to 16384
[2015-07-22 13:23:30] Pool 0 difficulty changed to 256
[2015-07-22 13:23:30] Network diff set to 1.9K
```

Fig. 1.12: Starting cgminer

As we can see, cgminer is running and it is connected to the pool we specified.

We will now briefly review the options that cgminer offers while it's running.

There are menu items for: **Pool management**, **GPU management**, **Settings**, and **Display options**. Let's examine them a little more closely. To get into a menu item, simply press the letter that corresponds to the item in question. The letters are wrapped in square brackets to indicate that they can be selected.

The following is the screenshot of **Pool management**:

```
Command Prompt - cgminer  -c C:\CRYPTO\cgminer-config\cgminer-multipo...   —  □  ×

_cgminer version 3.7.2 - Started: [2015-07-22 13:23:30]
-------------------------------------------------------------------
 (15s):326.5M (avg):346.2Mh/s | A:0  R:0  HW:0  WU:4.6/m
 ST: 2  SS: 0  NB: 1  LW: 27  GF: 0  RF: 0
 Connected to us-west.multipool.us diff 256 with stratum as user 0xfffff.280x
 Block: 1d4d1f7d...  Diff:1.9K  Started: [13:23:30]  Best share: 14
-------------------------------------------------------------------
 [P]ool management [G]PU management [S]ettings [D]isplay options [Q]uit
 GPU 0:  63.0C 1371RPM | 349.1M/401.0Mh/s | A:0 R:0 HW:0 WU: 6.1/m I:13
-------------------------------------------------------------------

0: Enabled Alive Quota 1 Prio 0: stratum+tcp://us-west.multipool.us:7777  User:0
xfffff.280x

Current pool management strategy: Failover
[F]ailover only enabled
Pool [A]dd [R]emove [D]isable [E]nable [Q]uota change
[C]hange management strategy [S]witch pool [I]nformation
Or press any other key to continue
```

Fig. 1.13: Pool management in cgminer

Here we can add more pools, remove ones we no longer need, disable, enable pools, or change the mining quota. We can also change our management strategy.

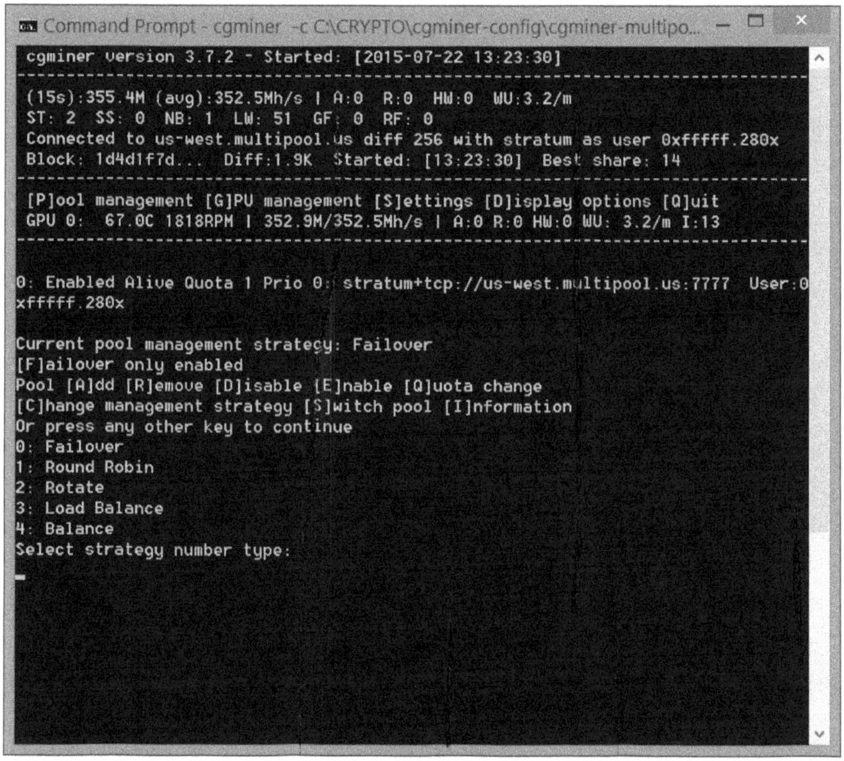

Fig. 1.14: Pool management strategy

As we can see, there are five options for pool management. We usually use the default option: `Failover`, which switches to the next pool in the case of the current pool's outage. These options are best explained in the `README` file that is included with cgminer.

The next option is **GPU management** — pressing *G* will bring up the following screen:

```
Command Prompt - cgminer  -c C:\CRYPTO\cgminer-config\cgminer-multipo...   —   □   ×

_cgminer version 3.7.2 - Started: [2015-07-22 13:23:30]
---------------------------------------------------------------------------
 (15s):354.2M (avg):352.8Mh/s | A:0  R:0  HW:0  WU:2.8/m
ST: 2  SS: 0  NB: 1  LW: 69  GF: 0  RF: 0
Connected to us-west.multipool.us diff 256 with stratum as user 0xfffff.280x
Block: 1d4d1f7d...  Diff:1.9K Started: [13:23:30]  Best share: 14
---------------------------------------------------------------------------
 [P]ool management [G]PU management [S]ettings [D]isplay options [Q]uit
 GPU 0:  68.0C 1973RPM | 354.9M/357.5Mh/s | A:0 R:0 HW:0 WU: 3.0/m I:13
---------------------------------------------------------------------------

GPU 0: 354.3 / 367.8 Mh/s | A:0  R:0  HW:0  U:0.00/m  I:13
68.0 C  F: 47% (1974 RPM)  E: 1000 MHz  M: 1400 Mhz  U: 1.206U  A: 99%  P: 0%
Last initialised: [2015-07-22 13:23:30]
Intensity: 13
Thread 0: 173.7 Mh/s Enabled ALIVE
Thread 1: 180.5 Mh/s Enabled ALIVE

[E]nable [D]isable [I]ntensity [R]estart GPU [C]hange settings
Or press any other key to continue
```

Fig. 1.15: GPU management screen

Here we can see the current statistics about our GPUs. The read-out shows temperature, fan speed, GPU clock, memory clock, and other information that maybe available for the particular hardware at hand. We can also manage our GPUs, in case we have multiple ones. We can disable or enable additional GPUs, change the intensity setting on each GPU, and change other settings as well.

Let's exit this menu (press space to exit) and go back to the main screen. Let's now look at the **Settings** menu. Pressing *S* will bring up the following screen:

```
Command Prompt - cgminer  -c C:\CRYPTO\cgminer-config\cgminer-multipo...   —   □   ×
cgminer version 3.7.2 - Started: [2015-07-22 13:23:30]
--------------------------------------------------------------------------------
(15s):355.2M (avg):351.8Mh/s | A:0  R:0  HW:0  WU:2.8/m
ST: 2  SS: 0  NB: 1  LW: 65  GF: 0  RF: 0
Connected to us-west.multipool.us diff 256 with stratum as user 0xfffff.280x
Block: 1d4d1f7d...  Diff:1.9K  Started: [13:23:30]  Best share: 14
--------------------------------------------------------------------------------
[P]ool management [G]PU management [S]ettings [D]isplay options [Q]uit
GPU 0:   67.0C 1974RPM | 356.1M/365.5Mh/s | A:0 R:0 HW:0 WU: 2.8/m I:13
--------------------------------------------------------------------------------

[Q]ueue: 1
[S]cantime: 60
[E]xpiry: 120
[W]rite config file
[C]gminer restart
Select an option or any other key to return
```

Fig. 1.16: Settings options in cgminer

Here, the most interesting option is `Write config file`. Pressing *W* will save a config file that we can use in the future to start cgminer with the appropriate settings. We will go into details in a later chapter – right now we want you to be aware that such an option exists, as it will prove useful.

Finally, the **Display option** from the main screen of cgminer will let us control what we want to see on the screen while cgminer is working. Pressing *D* will bring us to the following screen:

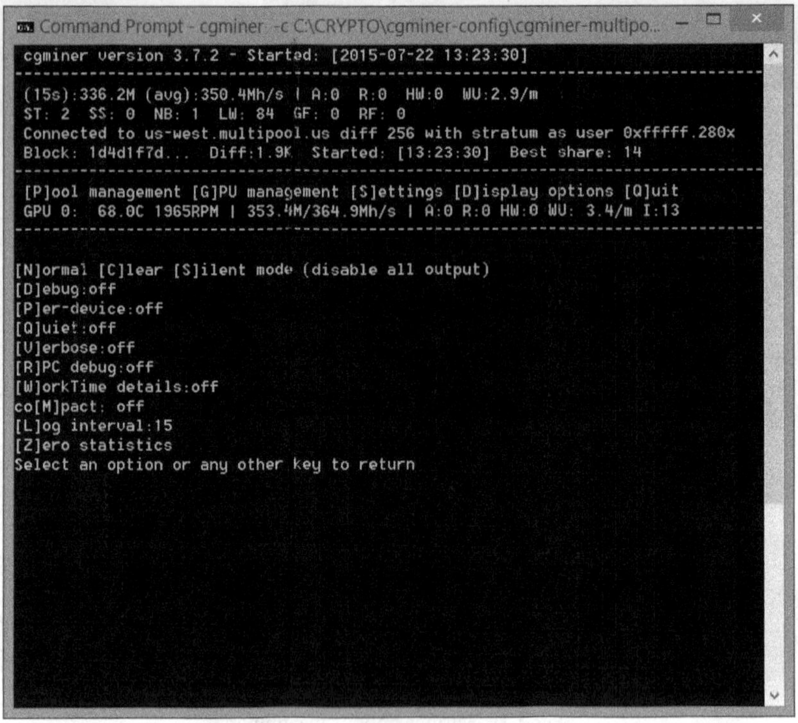

Fig. 1.17: Display options

We find that the default display options are sufficient for most miners. If you are interested in additional details, you may want to delve into the options by reading the README file that is shipped with cgminer. We do recommend everyone to at least skim through that file, as it is filled with useful information. We will touch upon the most important functions of the software later on, but a full description and explanation of all the features is beyond the scope of this book.

Finally, we should note that exiting cgminer, for whatever reason, can be accomplished by pressing *Q*.

Summary

In this chapter, we glanced at Bitcoin wallets and mining software. We examined the different flavors that wallets come in, from software wallets to hardware wallets. We looked at the difference between full wallets — ones that keep a full copy of the block chain, and thin client wallets that do not download the entire block chain but instead use a different technique to verify transactions. We also touched upon hosted wallets and wallet security was covered at a basic level. Always keep in mind that securing your wallet is an activity worth the effort.

Next, we looked at mining software. We discussed why such software is needed and what it accomplishes. We examined mining software by looking at one of the most popular: cgminer. We briefly discussed the options available when running cgminer.

This chapter was meant as a refresher — we will delve deeper into these topics in subsequent chapters. We hope that you found this chapter interesting and will stay with us for the rest of the journey.

2
CPU Mining

In this chapter, we will take a look at some actual mining. We will examine mining as it first started when Bitcoin was released. In those early days, the only way to mine was using the **Central Processing Unit** (**CPU**) on your computer and the Bitcoin Core wallet. We will explore mining with a Bitcoin wallet. Once you start mining, you can't help but feel as if you've been transported back to 2009 when Bitcoin was known to only a small group of enthusiasts. As time went by, multi-threaded software was written to take advantage of multiple cores of a CPU.

We will delve into the following topics in this chapter:

- CPU mining with Bitcoin Core
- CPU mining software
- Pros and cons of CPU mining
- Best practices when mining with CPUs
- Profitability of CPU mining

[In this chapter, we are using Ubuntu Linux and all the examples are for that OS.]

Mining with Bitcoin Core

The Bitcoin Core wallet has built-in capabilities for mining; therefore, it is really easy to use the wallet to mine on your machine. The wallet will use your CPU to mine. As you might recall, mining is basically hashing of a candidate block over and over again until the result is smaller than the current difficulty threshold.

To mine with your CPU and Bitcoin Core, open up the wallet software:

1. Now click on the **Help** menu and select **Debug Window**.

2. Then click on the **Console** tab—the console will appear. Remember, to see a list of all available commands, type `help` and press *Enter*.

The command to mine with your wallet is `setgenerate`. The syntax of the command is as follows:

```
setgenerate <true|false> <number of cores to be used>
```

To start mining with only 1 core, type `setgenerate true 1`:

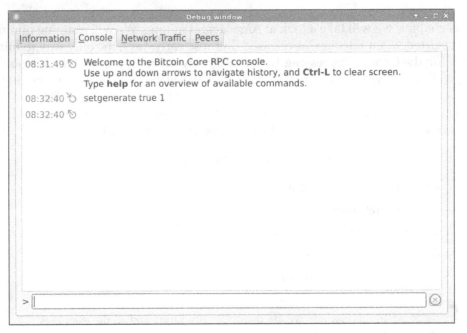

Fig. 2.1: Starting mining in Bitcoin Core

To make sure that your wallet is mining, you can go to your **Task Manager** in Windows, **Activity Monitor** in Mac OS, or **System Monitor** in Linux and see if one core is working at 100%.

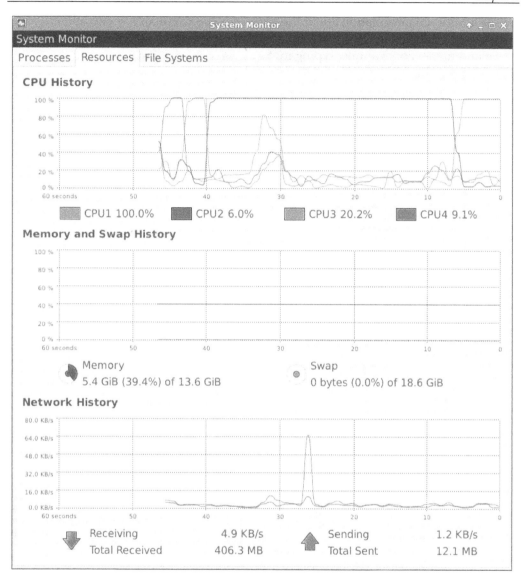

Fig. 2.2: Linux' System Monitor

As you can see, one core is always working at 100% capacity. You can try running `setgenerate` with more than one core to verify that additional cores will be working at 100%. To stop the mining process, type in the following into the Bitcoin Core wallet console:

```
setgenerate false
```

To see additional information about the `setgenerate` command or any other command in the Bitcoin Core software, you can type in `help` followed by the command name. For example, typing in: `help setgenerate` will give you the following output:

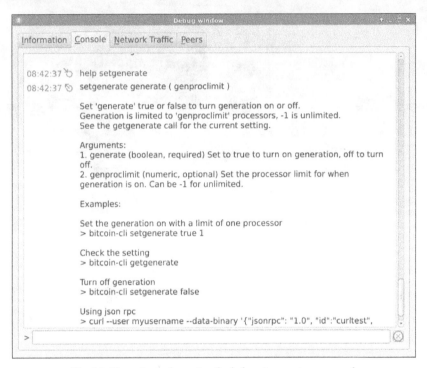

Fig. 2.3: The output of running the help setgenerate command

 In older Bitcoin Core clients, it was possible to see how fast your wallet was mining using the `gethashespersec` command. Since wallet-mining is no longer popular, that command has been removed and is no longer available. It is worth noting that the `gethashespersec` command is still available in some alt-coins wallets.

Since alt-coins are, for the most part, forks of Bitcoin, most of the discussion here regarding the Bitcoin Core wallet also translates to alt-coin wallets. So if you are really interested in seeing the number of hashes your CPU is generating, you can do that in an alt-coin wallet if you have one installed. If you do not have one, don't worry; we will show you another way to measure your CPU's hashing performance.

Definition

An alt-coin is another type of cryptocurrency that was created by copying and modifying Bitcoin's code. The most popular alt-coins are Litecoin, Dogecoin, and Namecoin. For a list of the biggest (by market capitalization) cryptocurrencies see http://coinmarketcap.com/.

Mining software

The most popular software to mine with your CPU is called **CPUMiner**. You can find the source code on GitHub at https://github.com/pooler/cpuminer. Precompiled binaries can be downloaded from https://sourceforge.net/projects/cpuminer/files/.

Once you have downloaded and extracted the software, the next step is to configure it. The easiest way to mine is to sign up for a mining pool, then you connect to the pool with your mining software and you're done. There are literally hundreds of mining pools. We recommend that you pick a well known pool that has been in existence for a little while. For our purpose, we will use a multipool.

A multipool is a pool that mines multiple coins, that is, it is not dedicated to one type of coin. These pools calculate which coin is the most profitable to mine and automatically switch your miner to mine that coin. We registered an account on a multipool with the URL: https://www.multipool.us for demonstration purposes.

The next step on any pool is to create a worker. A worker is simply a way to identify your hardware. If you are using two computers to mine, you would create two workers. Once you have your pool account and worker info set up on the pool, you are ready to start mining.

To see all the options of CPUMiner, do the following. In a terminal window, navigate to the directory from which you extracted CPUMiner; there is a file called `minerd`. Run the following command `./minerd --help` which will result in the following output:

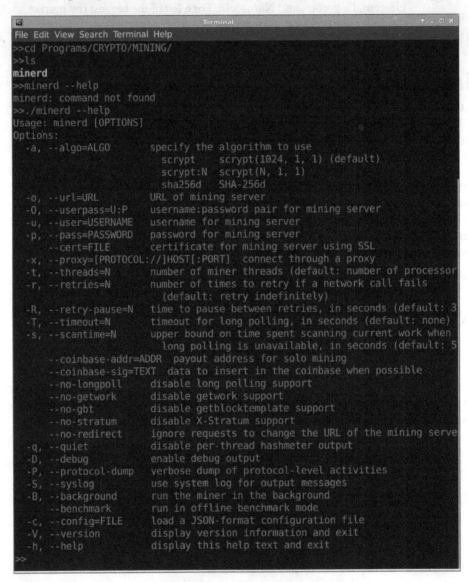

Fig. 2.4: Output of the minerd --help command

Let's start mining

To connect CPUMiner to a pool, you will need the following information:

- The URL of your pool
- The port number of the pool server
- Your mining pool username
- Your worker's name
- Your worker's password

Once you have all this information, you can run CPUMiner with the following options:

```
./minerd --url <poolurl:port> --userpass <USERNAME.WORKER:PASSWORD>
-a<algorithm>
```

As a concrete example, we will connect to the multipool, as shown:

```
./minerd --url stratum+tcp://us-west.multipool.us:9999 -a sha256d
--userpass bit.miner:x
```

If you have connected to your pool successfully, your screen will look similar to the following screen:

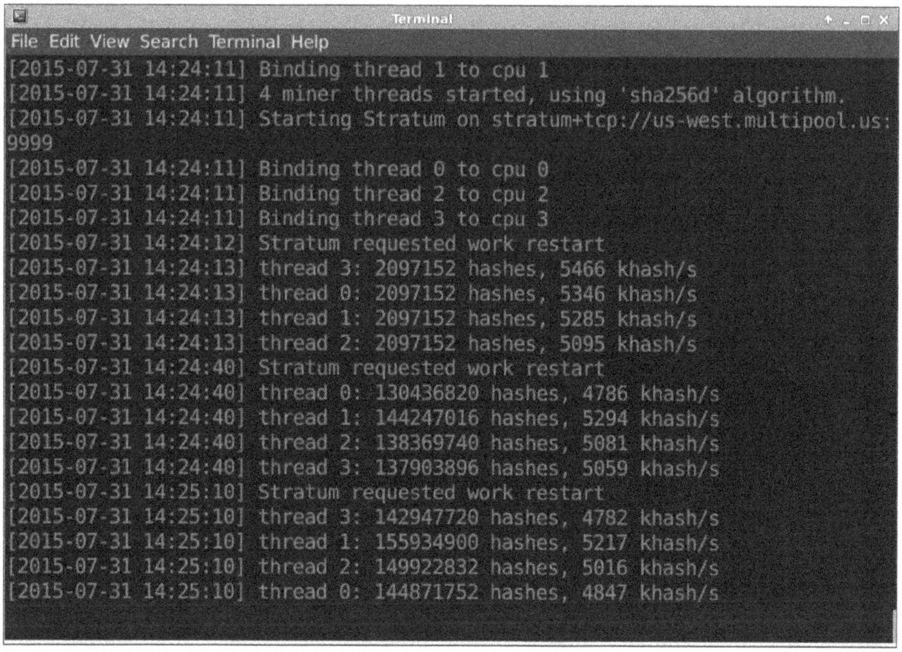

Fig. 2.5: CPUMiner working

You can see that our 4-core CPU can do about 5400 kilohashes per second (KH/s) on each core. In total, that is roughly 21000 KH/s or 21 megahashes per second (MH/s), 0.021 gigahashes per second (GH/s), or 0.000021 terahashes per second (TH/s). As you can imagine, that is a very small amount when compared to the total Bitcoin network hashing power. Currently, (at block # 391770) the network hashing power is 955,300 TH/s. Solo mining Bitcoin with a CPU will statistically take a long time before a block can be solved; however, there is a chance that you can get lucky and solve a block.

Pros and cons of mining

Mining with a CPU has its advantages and disadvantages. Let's examine these in order to understand better if and when it is appropriate to use your CPUs to mine Bitcoin. As you may recall in the beginning, everyone used a CPU to mine for bitcoins. Those days are long gone, but you can still mine on your CPU.

Pros of mining

CPU mining is very useful in the process of understanding mining. We strongly believe that's where every miner should start. You do not need any specialized hardware other than your computer. In the process of setting up the software, you will learn all the little tricks that are applicable to your hardware. You will also learn how the CPU will compare to more advanced hardware, such as GPUs and ASICs.

To summarize, we encourage you to try CPU mining for the following reasons:

- No specialized hardware required
- Very good starting point to enter mining
- Invaluable educational experience
- It is fun to mine

Cons of mining

CPU mining for Bitcoin is unfortunately no longer profitable. That is, it is highly unlikely that one could earn enough funds to cover the cost of electricity used up by the CPU in the process of mining. Even if electricity was free, the amount of coins earned while mining using a CPU would not cover the depreciation of the computer hardware. For example http://multipool.us posts profitability estimates.

As of Jan 04 2016, daily Bitcoin earnings are 500 satoshis per GH/s of hashing power. As you recall, our CPU was running at 0.021 GH/s. Therefore, its earnings would be approximately 11 satoshis per day, which at an exchange rate of 400 US Dollars (USD) per bitcoin translates to less than a penny a day. (Keep in mind that these are estimates only, in practice results will vary.)

[A satoshi is the smallest subunit of bitcoin. 1 satoshi = 0.00000001 bitcoin]

To summarize, we discourage continuous use of your CPUs for the purpose of mining for the following reasons:

- Electricity cost
- No longer profitable
- Constant wear and tear on your CPUs

Best practices when mining with CPUs

Let's look into the recommended things to do, when mining with CPUs. Although mining Bitcoin is no longer profitable with a CPU, mining other coins may bring in some profits. If you are going to use your CPU for mining, you might as well observe the practices that are going to make it easier and safer for you.

First, make sure that your computer has adequate cooling and the CPU fan is working along with all the other fans in your computer. Make sure your computer has adequate airflow around it. There should not be anything directly around or on top of your computer. Basically, you need good airflow. The reason is that, while mining, your CPU's cores will be running at 100%, which will generate a good amount of heat. If that heat is not dissipated by the fans, it may cause damage to your hardware.

Secondly, to get the most hashes out of your CPU, close all other programs running on your computer. If you are mining with a pool, have only the mining software open. If you are mining solo, you will also need to have your wallet open. Be aware that, if you are using your computer for any other purpose while mining, it will slow down the mining process.

Profitability of mining

As we have mentioned earlier, the Bitcoin network hash rate is really high now. Mining with a CPU is no longer guaranteed to bring in profits. This is due to the fact that, during the mining process, you are competing with other miners to try to solve a block. You will be at a disadvantage if those other miners are running faster hardware, as your hardware can only make a certain amount of guesses (hashes) in a given time frame.

To compare the mining speed of a few CPU's, look at the following table:

CPU	Mining speed (KH/s)	Power used (Watts)	# of cores
Athlon 64 X2 5600+	6.07	89	2
Athlon II X3 425	9.5	125	4
Phenom II X4 955	22	125	4
FX-8120	46	125	8
FX-8350	65	125	8
Core 2 Quad Q6600	9.68	100	4
Core 2 Quad Q9550	32.2	125	4
Core i3-2130	23	65	4
Core i5-2500K	48	90	4
Core i5-3570K	55	90	4
Core i7-3930K	98	200	12

Table. 2.1: Comparison of mining speed of CPUs

As you can see, CPU's do not hash very fast. The fastest in our list almost reaches 100 KH/s. Compared to the Bitcoin network, this is an extremely small amount of hashing power.

To calculate expected rewards from mining, we can do the following. First, calculate what percentage of total hashing power you command. To look up the network mining speed, execute the `getmininginfo` command in the console of the Bitcoin Core wallet. We will do our calculations with a CPU that can hash at *100 KH/s = 0.1 MH/s = 0.0001 GH/s = 0.0000001 TH/s.*

If the Bitcoin network hashes at 400,000 TH/s, our proportion of the hashing power is as follows:

```
0.0000001 / 400 000 = 0.00000000000025 of the total mining power
```

On average, a Bitcoin block is found every 10 minutes, so six per hour, and 144 for a 24-hour period. The current reward per block is 25 BTC; therefore, in a day we have *144*25 = 3600* BTC mined.

 If we command a certain percentage of the mining power, then on average we should earn that proportion of newly minted bitcoins.

Multiplying our portion of hashing power by the number of bitcoins minted daily we arrive at:

```
0.00000000000025 * 3600 = 0.0000000009
```

As we can see, it is less than the smallest unit of a bitcoin (which is called a satoshi and it is the 8th decimal place when dividing a bitcoin). Given the small profits to be made, it is no wonder that most people have stopped using their CPUs to mine for bitcoins.

Summary

In this chapter, we have looked at CPU mining. We looked at the easiest way to start mining – the built-in `setgenerate` function in the Bitcoin Core wallet. We delved into the most popular CPU mining software – CPUMiner. We showed you how to set it up and run it so that you can start mining.

We also touched upon the advantages and disadvantages of CPU mining. Consider those when deciding to mine. We also presented a set of good practices to keep in mind while running your mining process. They are common sense to most, but sometimes the most obvious things are forgotten. If you adhere to these practices, you should not encounter any problems while mining.

We also examined the profitability of CPU mining. We showed you a simple way of calculating, on average, your expected earnings. Even though CPU mining is no longer profitable, it is nevertheless a good educational experience.

In the next chapter, we will look at mining with your graphics card, commonly referred to as a **Graphics Processing Unit** (**GPU**). Mining with GPU's is simply called GPU mining.

3
GPU Mining

In this chapter, we will take a look at mining with **Graphic Processing Units** or **GPUs**. They are simply known as **Video Cards**. GPUs have a high degree of parallel processing built in and as such they are perfect for the repeated hashing of candidate blocks. That process is of course known as Bitcoin mining. GPUs can mine much faster than CPUs and hence are more desirable to a potential miner. In this chapter, we will cover the following topics:

- Setting up your wallet, mining software to allow GPU mining
- What happens when mining on the GPU?
- Benchmarks of mining speeds with different GPUs
- Pros and cons of GPU mining
- CPU versus GPU mining
- Best practices when mining with GPUs
- Discussion of profitability

Setting up a GPU for mining

In order to use a GPU to mine, you must have at least one GPU installed in your machine. At first, we will go over how to mine with only one GPU. Using multiple GPUs in your system to mine is a very a straightforward extension from mining with a single one.

Drivers

We will concentrate here on AMD GPUs as they offer the best hashing performance for the money when it comes to hashing power, the cost of the GPU, and electricity efficiency. Nvidia GPUs can also be used as long as you have the drivers for your video card installed.

 In order to mine with AMD GPUs, we will need the latest AMD drivers. You can find the latest AMD drivers here: `http://support.amd.com/en-us`.

If your GPU has already been installed in your machine, chances are that you have your driver installed already.

Here are some helpful Linux commands:

- `lspci | grep VGA`: This command displays the graphics cards in your system:

- `sudo aticonfig --adapter=all --odgt`: This command displays the graphics cards in your system and their current temperature. This command is also very useful if you have multiple GPUs in your system and would like to know if they are all detected or not:

```
Terminal                                              ↑ _ □ ×
File Edit View Search Terminal Help
>>sudo aticonfig --adapter=1 --odgt

Adapter 1 - AMD Radeon R9 200 Series
          Sensor 0: Temperature - 37.00 C
>>
```

- `cgminer -V`: This command prints out the cgminer version:

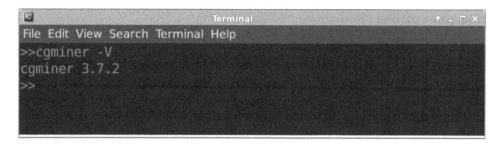

- `cgminer -n`: This command prints out information about software and hardware related to your GPUs:

```
>>cgminer -n
 [2016-01-07 15:10:18] CL Platform 0 vendor: Advanced Micro Devices, Inc.

 [2016-01-07 15:10:18] CL Platform 0 name: AMD Accelerated Parallel Processing

 [2016-01-07 15:10:18] CL Platform 0 version: OpenCL 2.0 AMD-APP (1642.5)

 [2016-01-07 15:10:18] Platform 0 devices: 2
 [2016-01-07 15:10:18]  0        Tahiti
 [2016-01-07 15:10:18]  1        Devastator
 [2016-01-07 15:10:18] GPU 0 AMD Radeon R9 200 Series              hardware mo
nitoring enabled
 [2016-01-07 15:10:18] GPU 1 AMD Radeon HD 8670D hardware monitoring enabled

 [2016-01-07 15:10:18] 2 GPU devices max detected
>>
```

Mining software

There are many mining programs out there. Our favorite is cgminer:

- The GitHub repository can be found at:
  https://github.com/ckolivas/cgminer
- Downloadable versions (for both Linux and Windows) can be found at the author's website at: http://ck.kolivas.org/apps/cgminer/
- Precompiled releases for MAC can be found at:
  http://spaceman.ca/cgminer/

The very last version to support GPU mining is 3.7.2. This is the version you want to download and install. Newer versions of cgminer do not support GPU mining, so make sure you download version 3.7.2.

Windows installation instructions

Cgminer can be downloaded as an executable file for Windows. Just unzip it and run it.

Linux installation instructions

These instructions are for the repository downloaded from the GitHub. You can use the following command to download the 3.7 branch from GitHub:

```
git clone -b 3.7 https://github.com/ckolivas/cgminer.git
```

We are assuming that you have Git installed on your machine; if not, you can install it by issuing the following command in a terminal:

```
sudo apt-get install git
```

The instructions are also included in the README file included with cgminer. We recommend reading the file to see if your machine has the required dependencies. In your terminal, execute the following commands:

```
cd cgminer-3.7.2
 ./autogen.sh
 ./configure --enable-opencl --enable-scrypt
```

If you are missing any dependencies, the configure script will let you know.

In our case, we need the `libncurses5-dev` build essentials and the `curl dev` libraries:

```
sudo apt-get install build-essential libcurl4-gnutls-dev  libncurses5-dev
```

Next, we will have to make sure that OpenCL is installed on our system. Once again the configure script will let us know if OpenCL is not present; we recommend downloading the AMD APP SDK. It can be found at:

```
http://developer.amd.com/tools-and-sdks/opencl-zone/amd-accelerated-
parallel-processing-app-sdk/
```

Download the appropriate one for your system, unzip it, and then run the installation script.

We will also download the ADL SDK library from here:

```
http://developer.amd.com/tools-and-sdks/graphics-development/display-
library-adl-sdk/
```

Unzip the downloaded file and copy the files in the include folder to the `cgminer/ADL_SDK` folder.

Let's run the configure script again:

`./configure -- enable-opencl -- enable-scrypt`

If it's successful, the output should look something like the following screenshot:

```
cgminer 3.7.2
--------------------------------------------------------------------


Configuration Options Summary:

  libcurl(GBT+getwork).: Enabled: -lcurl
  curses.TUI...........: FOUND: -lncurses
  OpenCL...............: FOUND. GPU mining support enabled
  scrypt...............: Enabled
  ADL..................: SDK found, GPU monitoring support enabled

  Avalon.ASICs.........: Disabled
  BFL.ASICs............: Disabled
  KnC.ASICs............: Disabled
  BitForce.FPGAs.......: Disabled
  BitFury.ASICs........: Disabled
  Hashfast.ASICs.......: Disabled
  BlackArrow.ASICs.....: Disabled
  Icarus.ASICs/FPGAs...: Disabled
  Klondike.ASICs.......: Disabled
  ModMiner.FPGAs.......: Disabled

Compilation...........: make (or gmake)
  CPPFLAGS.............:
  CFLAGS...............: -g -O2
  LDFLAGS..............:  -lpthread
  LDADD................: -ldl -lcurl    compat/jansson-2.5/src/.libs/libjansso
.a -lpthread -lOpenCL    -lm  -lrt

Installation..........: make install (as root if needed, with 'su' or 'sudo'
  prefix...............: /usr/local

>>
```

We enabled the `scrypt` algorithm in case you want to mine some alt-coins in the future. Now, let's build and install cgminer:

```
sudo make install
```

(You can try without `sudo`, but most likely the installation will fail as the installer won't be able to write to system folders).

Once you install cgminer, you can test which version you have by typing `cgminer -v` (make sure the `v` is capital) in your terminal. To see all the options that you can use with cgminer, type in `cgminer -h`.

> There are a lot of options that can overwhelm a new user; do not worry, we will go over the most important ones. To see an explanation of the commands, you can also read the README file included with cgminer. In fact, it is a good idea to skim through that file. You will learn a lot of useful information.

Once you have installed cgminer the next step is to configure it. The easiest way to mine is to sign up for a mining pool, then you connect to the pool with your mining software and you're done. There are literally hundreds of mining pools. We recommend that you pick a well known pool that has been in existence for a little while. For our purpose here, we will use a multipool. A multipool is a pool that mines multiple coins; in other words it is not dedicated to one type of coin. These pools calculate which coin is the most profitable to mine and automatically switch your miner to mine that coin.

> We registered an account on
> `https://www.multipool.us` for demonstration purposes.

The next step on any pool is to create a worker. A worker is simply a way to identify your hardware. If you are using two computers to mine, you will have to create two workers. Once you have your pool account and worker info set up on the pool, you are ready to start mining.

Let's start mining

To connect cgminer to a pool, you will need some information:

- The URL of your pool
- The port number of the pool server
- Your mining pool username

- Your worker's name
- Your worker's password

Once you have all this information, you can run cgminer with the following options:

For Linux machines, you can use the following command:

```
cgminer --url <poolurl:port> --userpass <USERNAME.WORKER:PASSWORD>
```

We can also use the short option identification:

```
cgminer -o <poolurl:port> -O <USERNAME.WORKER:PASSWORD>
```

As a concrete example, we would connect to the multipool, as shown:

```
cgminer -o stratum+tcp://us-west.multipool.us:9999 -O bit.miner:x
```

Cgminer connected to a pool and mining with 1 GPU (Windows OS) is shown in the following screenshot:

For completeness, we used the following command to start mining:

```
cgminer -o stratum+tcp://us-west.multipool.us:9999 -u <user.worker> -p x
-I 11 --worksize 512
```

We will go over the following options:

- `-I 11`: For intensity of GPU scanning, generally a higher number is better but there is a point at which it does not bring any increase in hashing speed. It is best to experiment with this setting and see the results. In addition, if you have only one GPU that also runs your displays, then changing the intensity may crash your desktop graphics or at least slow them down.

- `--worksize 512`: Worksize is another GPU-specific option. A quick web search will reveal what the setting should be for your particular GPUs (for example: `https://en.bitcoin.it/wiki/Non-specialized_hardware_comparison` or `https://litecoin.info/Mining_hardware_comparison`).

As you can see, our example GPU (Radeon R9 270x) can do about 400 MH/s. That is 0.4 GH/s or 0.0004 TH/s. As you can imagine, that is a very small amount when compared to the total Bitcoin network hashing power. Currently (at block # 370,000) the network hashing power is about 380,000 TH/s. Solo-mining Bitcoin with this GPU will take a long time before a block can be solved.

Multiple GPU setup

If you have multiple GPUs connected to your machine, you can use them all at the same time for mining. Cgminer lets us set up each GPU with different options. In order to do that, it is best to use a configuration file to give cgminer all the information. Once we have the configuration file, we start cgminer with the `--config` option to read in the file:

```
cgminer --config <configuration filename>
```

The following is a sample cgminer configuration file for multiple GPUs:

```
{
"pools" : [
  {
    "url" : "<pool url>",
    "user" : "me",
    "pass" : "x"
      },
  {
    "url" : "<pool url>",
    "user" : "me.280x",
```

```
        "pass" : "x"
      },
      {
        "url" : "<pool url>",
        "user" : "me.270x",
        "pass" : "x"
          }
      ],

  "intensity" : "16,18,19",
  "worksize" : "512",
  "gpu-engine" : "0-1010",
  "gpu-memclock" : "1450-1490",
  "lookup-gap" : "2",
  "failover-only" : true,
  "kernel-path" : "/usr/local/bin"


  }
```

The configuration file presented earlier is a configuration file for three AMD ATI Radeon 270x video cards. The intensity setting is different for each card. We set it at 16 for GPU0 because that GPU also runs the display on that machine. GPU1 has a setting of 18 because, physically, it was in the middle of the three GPUS. GPU2 has an intensity setting of 19 because it was on the outside of the three GPUs and as a result it was very well ventilated. As you can see, you can just comma-separate the values so that each GPU has its own setting. In other words we can customize the settings for each GPU individually.

Also, it is worth noting that we specified multiple pools in the configuration file so that, if one pool goes down, cgminer will switch to the next available pool. The switching is specified by the following option:

```
  "failover-only" : true
```

Mining on a GPU

As you might remember from *Chapter 1, Bitcoin Wallets and Mining Software*, mining is all about hashing a candidate block and seeing if the hash meets certain difficulty criteria. On a CPU, we could only run as many threads as we had cores to do our mining. Theoretically, we can run any number of threads but there is no advantage (as a matter of fact there is a disadvantage) in running more threads than the available number of cores. In contrast, video cards have been designed to run hundreds, even thousands, of threads and they have the hardware to support this massive thread concurrency.

When you are mining with a GPU, the mining software creates enough work to keep all the threads busy. Now, the GPU is hashing in parallel at the same time. The end result is that a GPU can perform many times more hashes than a CPU can. The mining software monitors all this work to make sure a valid solution, when found, is reported to the pool (when pool mining) or to the wallet (when solo mining). We will talk about both solo and pool mining in detail in later chapters.

Pros and cons of GPU mining

Mining with GPUs has its advantages and disadvantages. Let's examine these in order to better understand if and when it is appropriate to use your GPUs to mine Bitcoin. As you may recall, in the beginning everyone used a CPU to mine bitcoins; then clever people figured out how to do it on GPUs.

Pros of GPU mining

GPU mining is the second step in the mining evolution (first there was CPU mining); it's very useful in the process of understanding mining. We strongly believe that every miner should try mining with a GPU to experience how changing different options affects the speed and efficiency of GPU mining. Most likely, you already have a GPU in your desktop machine. In the process of setting up the software, you will learn all the little tricks that are applicable to your hardware. You will also learn how the GPU compares to more advanced hardware, such as FPGAs and ASICs.

To summarize, we encourage you to try GPU mining for the following reasons:

- If you have a video card in your system, then you need no additional hardware
- It's an invaluable educational experience
- It is fun to mine

Cons of GPU mining

GPU mining suffers from the same problems as CPU mining. GPU mining for Bitcoin is unfortunately no longer profitable. In other words, it is highly unlikely that we could earn enough funds to cover the cost of electricity used up by GPUs in the process of mining. Even if electricity was free, the amount of coins earned while mining using a GPU will not cover the depreciation of the computer hardware. For example, `https://www.multipool.us/` posts profitability estimates. As of Jan 06 2016, daily Bitcoin earnings are 800 satoshis per GH/s of hashing power. As you recall, our GPU was running at 0.4 GH/s. Therefore, its earnings will be 200 satoshis per day, which at $400 per Bitcoin translates to less than a penny a day.

To summarize, we discourage continuous use of your GPUs for the purpose of mining bitcoin for the following reasons:

- Electricity cost
- GPUs create a large amount of heat
- No longer profitable
- Constant wear and tear on your GPUs

 GPU mining can be profitable with alt-coins, but that discussion is beyond the scope of this book. See our upcoming *Mining Alt-Coins* book for more information.

Best practices when mining with GPUs

Let's look into recommended practices when mining with GPUs. Although mining Bitcoin is no longer profitable with GPUs, mining other coins may bring in some profits. If you are going to use your GPUs for mining, you might as well observe practices that are going to make it easier and safer for you.

First, make sure that your GPUs have adequate cooling and the GPU fans are at least two inches away from any other object. If your GPU is inside a desktop case, it is better to leave the case open. If you are building a mining rig with multiple GPUs, it is a good idea to add external fans to increase the airflow. It is also wise to leave the GPUs exposed (as in not enclosed), so that there is better air circulation. Remember that hot air rises, so it is best not to have anything above your mining rig. As you may have seen, people do use "milk crates" as enclosures for their mining rigs; it is a good starting point. However, now there are professional manufacturers of GPU mining rig frames.

 It is not unheard of for people to actually use their mining rigs as heating devices. Might as well benefit from the side effect.

Secondly, to get the most hashes out of your GPUs, experiment with the different settings. Once again, people do post their optimal settings online and it is not difficult to find them for your particular GPU or GPUs. However, if you are mining with a GPU that you are also using as a video card for your display, you won't get the optimal hashing power, as some of the GPU cycles are spent on the graphics display.

If you are thinking about purchasing GPUs for mining purposes, make sure that you calculate the cost per hash and also electricity used per hash. In mining, electricity is the biggest cost after hardware and it will exceed the cost of the hardware over time.

Benchmarks of mining speeds with different GPUs

As we mentioned earlier, the Bitcoin network hash rate is really high now. Mining with GPUs is no longer guaranteed to bring profits. This is due to the fact that during the mining process you are competing with other miners to try to solve a block. If those other miners are running on faster hardware, you will be at a disadvantage, as your hardware can only make a certain number of guesses (hashes) in a given time frame.

To compare the mining speed of a few GPU's, look at the following table:

GPU	Mining speed (MH/s)	Power used (Watts)
AMD 4870	90	150
AMD 5770	240	100
AMD 5830	300	125
AMD 5850	400	180
AMD 5870	480	200
AMD 5970	800	350
AMD 6990	800	400
NVIDIA GT-210	4	30
NVIDIA GTX-280	60	230
NVIDIA GTX-480	140	250
NVIDIA Tesla S1070	155	800
NVIDIA Tesla S2070	750	900

Table: 3.1: Comparison of mining speed of GPUs

GPU versus CPU mining

As you can see from a comparison between *Table 3-1* and *Table 2-1*, GPUs hash much faster than CPUs. The fastest in our list reaches 800 MH/s. This is a significant improvement over various CPUs and is due to the massively parallel nature of graphics cards. Even though GPUs mine much faster than CPUs, the mining speed of a GPU compared to the total mining power of the Bitcoin network is still just a tiny percentage of the total.

Profitability of GPU mining

To calculate expected rewards from mining, we can do the following. First, calculate what percentage of total hashing power you command. To look up the network mining speed, execute the `getmininginfo` command in the console of the Bitcoin Core wallet. We will do our calculations with a GPU that can hash at *1 GH/s = 0.1 TH/s*. If the Bitcoin network hashes at 400,000 TH/s, then our proportion of the hashing power is:

```
0.1 / 400 000 = 0.00000025 of the total mining power
```

On average, a Bitcoin block is found every 10 minutes; it amounts to six per hour and 144 for a 24-hour period. The current reward per block is 25 BTC; therefore, in a day we have *144*25 = 3600* BTC mined.

If we command a certain percentage of the mining power, then on average we should earn that proportion of the newly minted bitcoins.

Multiplying our portion of hashing power by the number of bitcoins minted daily we arrive at:

```
0.00000025 * 3600 BTC = 0.0009 BTC
```

As we can see, this is less than $0.25 USD for a 24-hour period.

Given the small profits to be made, it is no wonder that most people have stopped using their GPUs to mine for bitcoin. (Keep in mind that mining for alt-coins with your GPUs can still be profitable.)

Summary

In this chapter, we have looked at GPU mining, setting up the required mining software, and at certain GPU settings. We delved into the most popular GPU mining software—cgminer. We showed you how to set it up and run it, so that you can start mining by connecting to a pool.

We touched upon the advantages and disadvantages of GPU mining. You can consider those when you decide to mine. We also presented a set of good practices to keep in mind while running your mining process. They are common sense to most but sometimes the most obvious things are forgotten. If you adhere to those practices, you should not encounter any problems while mining.

We also examined the profitability of GPU mining. We showed you a simple way of calculating, on average, your expected earnings. Even though GPU mining is no longer profitable, it is nevertheless a good educational experience.

In the next chapter, we will look at mining with more specialized hardware built for mining.

4
FPGA Mining

In this chapter, we will take a look at mining with **Field-Programmable Gate Arrays** (**FPGAs**). They are microprocessors that can be programmed for a specific purpose. In the case of Bitcoin mining, they are configured to perform the SHA-256 hash function that is used in Bitcoin. FPGAs have a slight advantage over using GPUs for mining. The period of FPGA mining of Bitcoin was rather short (just under a year), as faster machines soon became available. The advent of ASIC technology for Bitcoin mining compelled a lot of miners to make the move from FPGAs to ASICs. Nevertheless, FPGA mining is worth learning about.

We will take a look at the following topics:

- Setting up mining software and drivers to allow FPGA mining
- What happens when mining on an FPGA
- Benchmarks of mining speeds with different FPGAs
- Pros and cons of FPGA mining
- FPGA versus other hardware mining
- The best practices when mining with FPGAs
- Discussion of profitability

Setup and installation of the required software

In order to mine with an FPGA miner, we need to connect and configure it with a controlling computer. Most FPGAs connect to a computer via USB; therefore, we can usually connect a large number of FPGAs to a single computer using USB hubs. We will, of course, need the appropriate software and drivers to mine with our FPGAs.

Mining software

There are many mining programs out there. Our favorite is **cgminer**. Its GitHub repository can be found at https://github.com/ckolivas/cgminer.

The downloadable versions (for both Linux and Windows) can be found at the author's website at http://ck.kolivas.org/apps/cgminer.

The precompiled releases for MAC can be found at http://spaceman.ca/cgminer/.

We recommend using the latest version of cgminer to mine with FPGAs, the current (August 2015) version is 4.9.2, it has support for both BitForce and ModMiner FPGAs.

Linux installation instructions

The author of cgminer provides built software that is ready for distribution. Download the appropriate file for your machine, unzip it, and the software is ready to use. You can test the version you have by typing cgminer -V (capital V) in your terminal, as shown in the following screenshot:

```
>>
>>
>>
>>cd ~/Programs/Cgminer/
>>cd cgminer-4.9.2-x86_64-built/
>>./cgminer -V
cgminer 4.9.2
>>
```

Fig. 4.1: Checking the version number of cgminer on Ubuntu

It is worthwhile to read through the FPGA-README file that comes with cgminer. A lot of useful knowledge and details are in that file. In case cgminer cannot see your FPGAs, there are instructions in the FPGA-README file for both Windows and Linux to fix that issue. We will not bother to reproduce them here in their entirety, but instead refer you to the FPGA-README file.

In summary, on Linux there maybe some permission issues. You can solve these by mining as root (start cgminer with the sudo command) or by making a regular user a member of the plugdev group:

```
sudo usermod -G plugdev -a <user_name>
```

If your system does not have such a group, you can create it with the following command:

```
sudo groupadd plugdev
```

To make things easier, the cgminer distribution includes a file called `01-cgminer.rules`. By copying the file onto your Linux system, you will make the FPGA miners members of the `plugdev` group. Use the following command to copy the file:

```
sudo cp 01-cgminer.rules /etc/udev/rules.d/
```

After rebooting your system, the changes should take effect. Check if cgminer sees your hardware by running the `cgminer -n` command.

Let's quickly check if we can mine by connecting to a pool. In the terminal, type:

```
./cgminer -o <poolurl:port> -O <USERNAME.WORKER:PASSWORD>
```

In our specific case, we will use the following parameters:

```
./cgminer -o stratum+tcp://us-west.multipool.us:9999 -O bit.miner:x
```

If everything is configured we will see cgminer working and using our FPGA to hash.

Windows installation instructions

Download the Windows version of cgminer. Currently it is the `cgminer-4.9.2-windows.zip` file. Unzip it and you're ready to configure the software and drivers. On Windows, in order to use some FPGAs, we need to change the drivers; we do not want to use the default Windows driver. We can use the zadig utility to accomplish this. To download zadiq go to `http://zadig.akeo.ie/`, we are using `zadiq_2.1.2.exe`.

1. Run zadig as administrator (right-click, select **Run as Administrator**).
    ° Navigate to **Options | List all devices**
    ° Choose your device from list
    ° Select **WinUSB** driver
    ° Click **Replace Driver**

2. After installation, you should receive the following message:

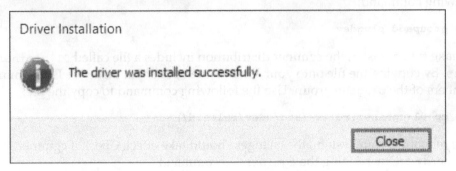

Fig. 4.2: Installation was successful

- ○ The new driver associated will be shown
- ○ Unplug and replug USB miner
- ○ Run `cgminer -n` to check if the mining device is seen by cgminer

Once you have downloaded and extracted the software and set up the drivers, it is time to test if everything is working. Try connecting to your favorite mining pool with cgminer, and if everything is configured correctly you should be mining away.

To be consistent, we will use `https://www.multipool.us` for demonstration purposes.

Let's start mining

Let's test our mining hardware, software, and drivers by connecting cgminer to a mining pool to see if everything is configured correctly. To connect cgminer to a pool you will need, as usual, the following relevant information.

- The URL of your pool
- The port number of the pool server
- Your mining pool username
- Your worker's name
- Your worker's password

Once you have all this information, you will run cgminer with the following options:

`cgminer --url <poolurl:port> --userpass <USERNAME.WORKER:PASSWORD>`

We can also use the short option identification, as shown:

`cgminer -o <poolurl:port> -O <USERNAME.WORKER:PASSWORD>`

As a concrete example, we will connect to the multipool, as shown:

```
cgminer -o stratum+tcp://us-west.multipool.us:9999 -O bit.miner:x
```

What happens when mining on a FPGA

As you can recall, from *Chapter 1, Bitcoin Wallets and Mining Software*, mining is all about hashing a candidate block and seeing if the hash meets certain difficulty criteria. On a CPU we could only run as many threads as we had cores to do our mining. On a GPU we can run hundreds or thousands of threads, thereby, speeding up our computations. However, both the CPU and GPU are designed for multi-purpose, universal computing. This means that both can execute any valid code; in computing terms this is called **Turing-completeness**. On the other hand, FPGAs are programmed for a specific purpose. The advantage lies in being able to optimize the hardware for the task required. This is the reason why FPGAs are faster than the best GPUs at performing hashing calculations.

When mining with an FPGA, the mining software creates the necessary work, and the FPGA hashes away to find a possible solution. The mining software monitors all this work to make sure that a valid solution, when found, is reported to the pool (when pool mining) or to the wallet (when solo mining). Don't worry; we will talk about both solo and pool mining in detail in later chapters.

Pros and cons of FPGA mining

Mining with FPGAs has its advantages and disadvantages. Let's examine these in order to understand if and when it is appropriate to use FPGAs to mine Bitcoin. As you may recall, mining started on CPUs and then it moved over to GPUs; then people discovered that FPGAs could be used for mining as well.

Pros of FPGA mining

FPGA mining is the third step in mining hardware evolution. They are faster and more efficient than GPUs.

To summarize, mining Bitcoin with FPGAs has the following advantages:

- FPGAs are faster than GPUs and CPUs
- FPGAs are more electricity-efficient, per unit of hashing, than CPUs or GPUs

Cons of FPGA mining

FPGAs are rather difficult to source and program, and are not usually sold in stores open to the public. We have not touched upon programming FPGAs for Bitcoin mining, as we assumed you have acquired pre-programmed FPGAs. There are several good resources on the Internet regarding FPGA programming; electricity cost is also an issue with FPGAs, although not to the same extent as with GPUs.

To summarize, mining Bitcoin with FPGAs has the following disadvantages:

- Electricity cost
- Hardware costs
- Fierce competition with other miners

Best practices when mining with FPGAs

Let's look into the recommended things to do when mining with FPGAs. Mining is fun and it can also be profitable if several factors are taken into account.

Make sure that all your FPGAs have adequate cooling. Additional fans beyond what is provided by the manufacturer are always a good idea. Remove dust frequently, as a build up of dust might have a detrimental effect on cooling efficiency and hence, mining speed.

For your particular mining machine, search online for all the optimization tweaks to get all the hashing power that is possible. However, due to a large variety of mining machines, we cannot provide all the possible tweaks in our book.

When setting up a mining operation for profit, keep in mind that the electricity cost will be a large percentage of your overall cost; hence, seek a location with the lowest electricity rates. Think about cooling costs; perhaps it will be the most beneficial to mine where the climate is cooler.

When purchasing FPGAs, make sure that you calculate hashes per dollar of hardware costs and also hashes per unit of electricity used. In mining, electricity is the biggest cost after hardware, and electricity will exceed the cost of the hardware over time. Keep in mind that hardware costs fall over time; so, purchasing your equipment in stages, rather than all at once, may be desirable.

To summarize, keep in mind the following factors when mining with FPGAs:

- Adequate cooling
- Optimization
- Electricity costs
- Hardware cost per MH/s

Benchmarks of mining speeds with different FPGAs

As we have mentioned earlier, the Bitcoin network hash rate is really high now, and even mining with FPGAs does not guarantee profits. This is due to the fact that during the mining process you are competing with other miners to try to solve a block. If those other miners are running a larger percentage of the total mining power, you will be at a disadvantage, as they are more likely to solve a block.

To compare the mining speed of a few FPGAs, look at the following table:

FPGA	Mining speed MH/s	Power used watts	Efficiency W/MH/s
Bitcoin Dominator X5000	100	6.8	0.068
Icarus	380	19.2	0.051
Lancelot	400	26	0.065
ModMiner Quad	800	40	0.05
Butterflylabs Mini Rig	25,200	1250	0.05

Table 4.1: Comparison of mining speed of different FPGAs

FPGA versus GPU and CPU mining

As you can see, from a comparison between table 4.1 and tables 3.1 and 2.1, FPGAs hash much faster than any other hardware. The fastest in our list reaches 25,000 MH/s. FPGAs are faster at performing hashing calculations than both CPUs and GPUs. They are also more efficient as measured by the use of electricity per hashing unit. The increase in hashing speed in FPGAs is a significant improvement over GPUs and even more so over CPUs.

Profitability of FPGA mining

In calculating your potential profit, keep in mind the following factors:

- The cost of your FPGAs
- Electricity costs to run the hardware
- Cooling costs—FPGAs generate a decent amount of heat
- Your percentage of the total network hashing power

To calculate expected rewards from mining, we can do the following. First calculate what percentage of total hashing power you command. To look up the network mining speed, execute the `getmininginfo` command in the console of the Bitcoin Core wallet. We will do our calculations with an FPGA that can hash at 1GH/s (which is 0.001 TH/s). If the Bitcoin network hashes at 400000 TH/s, then our proportion of the hashing power is *0.001/400000=0.0000000025* of the total mining power.

A Bitcoin block is found on an average of every 10 minutes, so six per hour and 144 for a 24-hour period. The current reward per block is 25 BTC; therefore, in a day we have *144*25=3600* BTC mined.

If we command a certain percentage of the mining power, then on an average we should earn that proportion of newly minted bitcoins.

Multiplying our portion of hashing power by the number of bitcoins minted daily, we arrive at: *0.0000000025*3600 BTC=0.000009 BTC*

As one can see that is roughly $0.0025 USD for a 24-hour period.

For up-to-the-day profitability you can visit `https://www.multipool.us/`, which publishes the average profitability per gigahash of mining power.

Summary

In this chapter, we explored FPGA mining. We explained how to install the mining software and how to set up the appropriate drivers. Cgminer was our software of choice. We set it up on both Linux and Windows operating systems. We also connected to a mining pool to make sure everything was working as planned.

We examined the advantages and disadvantages of mining with FPGAs. It would serve any miner well to ponder these when deciding to start mining, or when thinking about improving current mining operations. We touched upon the best practices that we recommend keeping in mind.

We also investigated the profitability of mining, given current conditions. A simple way of calculating, on average, your earnings was also presented. We concluded that mining competition is fierce; therefore, any improvements you can make will serve you well.

In the next chapter, we will look at mining with the fastest technology available — ASICs.

5
ASIC Mining

In this chapter, we will take a look at mining with **Application Specific Integrated Circuits** or **ASICs**. They are microprocessors built for a single purpose. In the case of Bitcoin mining, they are built to perform the SHA-256 hash function that is used in Bitcoin. ASICs have a clear advantage over other mining hardware, as they are the fastest hashing machines (save for the still-theoretical quantum computer) designed specifically for the repeated hashing of candidate blocks.

ASICs can mine much faster than CPUs, GPUs, and FPGAs and are therefore more desirable to a potential miner. Furthermore, improvements in ASIC technology mean that even faster machines have been hitting the market in the last two years. However, the trend cannot continue forever; there is a limit to the hashing speed of an ASIC chip.

This is perhaps the most exciting chapter in our book. A vast majority of mining is currently conducted on ASICs; therefore, this chapter is extremely relevant to today's mining techniques. In this chapter we will cover the following topics:

- Setting up mining software and drivers to allow ASIC mining
- Pros and cons of ASIC mining
- The best practices when mining with ASICs
- Discussion about profitability
- ASICs versus other mining hardware

Setting up mining software

In order to mine with an ASIC miner, we need to connect and configure it with a controlling computer. Most ASICs connect to a computer via a USB; therefore, with the use of USB hubs we can usually connect a large number of ASICs to a single computer. We will, of course, need the appropriate software and drivers to use our ASICs to mine.

Drivers

We will present our tests here using a **Butterfly Labs (BFL)** ASIC; however, most popular ASICs connect and configure the same way.

Mining software

There are many mining programs out there. Our favorite is cgminer. The GitHub repository can be found at: `https://github.com/ckolivas/cgminer`. The downloadable versions (for both Linux and Windows) can be found at the author's website: `http://ck.kolivas.org/apps/cgminer`.

We recommend using the latest version of cgminer to mine with ASICs; currently, (August 2015) the latest version is version 4.9.2.

> Note that the version of cgminer that we used for GPU mining was an earlier version: 3.7.2. As a result, an installation of the latest version will be required.

Installing cgminer on Linux

The author of cgminer provides built software that is ready for distribution. Download the appropriate file for your machine, unzip it, and the software is ready to use.

You can test which version you have by typing `cgminer -V` on your terminal.

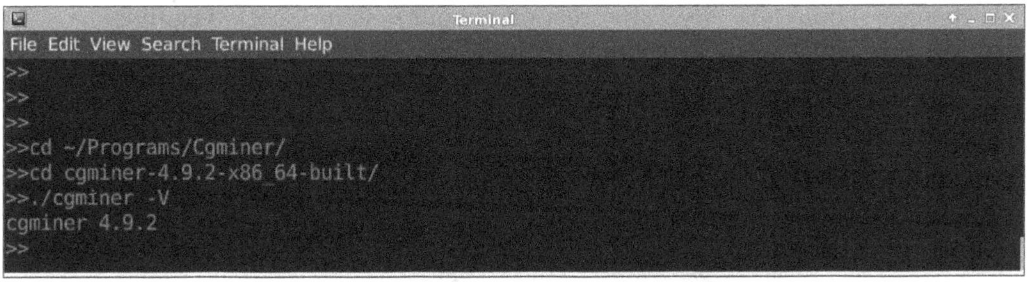

Fig. 5.1: checking the version number of cgminer on Ubuntu

It is very worthwhile to read through the ASIC-README file, which comes with cgminer. A lot of useful knowledge and details are in that file. In case cgminer cannot see your ASICs, there are instructions in the ASIC-README file for both Windows and Linux to fix that issue. We will not bother reproducing them here in their entirety, but instead refer the reader to take a look at the ASIC-README file.

In summary, on Linux there maybe some permission issues, and you can solve these by mining as root (start cgminer with the sudo command) or by making a regular user a member of the plugdev group, as shown:

```
sudo usermod -G plugdev -a <user_name>
```

If your system does not have such a group, you can create it with the following command:

```
sudo groupadd plugdev
```

To make things easier, the cgminer distribution includes a file called 01-cgminer. rules. By copying the file onto your Linux system, you will make BFL miners be part of the plugdev group; use the following command to copy the file:

```
sudo cp 01-cgminer.rules /etc/udev/rules.d/
```

The changes should take effect after rebooting your system. Check if cgminer recognizes your hardware by running the `cgminer -n` command:

```
Terminal
File Edit View Search Terminal Help
>>cd ~/Programs/Cgminer/cgminer-4.9.2-x86_64-built/
>>./cgminer -n
 [2015-08-30 15:59:05] USB all: found 13 devices - listing known devices
.USB dev 0: Bus 2 Device 2 ID: 0403:6014
  Manufacturer: 'Butterfly Labs'
  Product: 'BitFORCE SHA256 SC'
 [2015-08-30 15:59:05] 1 known USB devices
>>
```

Fig. 5.2: checking if cgminer sees the mining hardware connected to the computer

Let's quickly check if we can mine by connecting to a pool. In the terminal, type:

`./cgminer -o <poolurl:port> -O <USERNAME.WORKER:PASSWORD>`

In our case, it should be as follows:

`./cgminer -o stratum+tcp://us-west.multipool.us:9999 -O bit.miner:x`

If everything is configured, we will see cgminer working and using our ASIC to hash.

Installing cgminer on Windows

Download the Windows version of cgminer. Currently it will be the `cgminer-4.9.2-windows.zip` file. Unzip it and you're ready to configure the software and drivers. For Windows, in order to use the ASICs, we need to change the drivers. We do not want to use the default Windows driver. We can use the **zadig** utility to accomplish that. Download zadig (you can find it at: `http://zadig.akeo.ie/`), as we are going to move ahead with `zadig_2.1.2.exe`:

1. Run zadig as an administrator (right click, select **Run as Administrator**) then do the following:
   - ° Navigate to **Options | List all devices**
   - ° Choose a device from the list (for example **BitFORCE SHA256 SC**)
   - ° Select the **WinUSB** driver
   - ° Click on **Replace Driver**

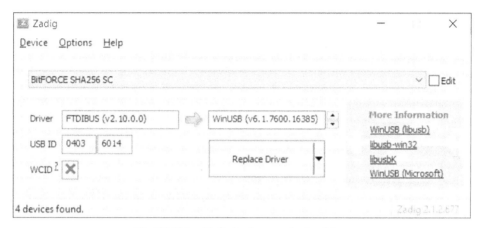

Fig. 5.3: Using Zadig to change a device driver

2. After installation, you should receive the following message:

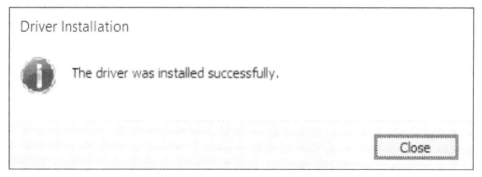

Fig. 5.4: installation was successful

3. The new driver associated will be as shown:

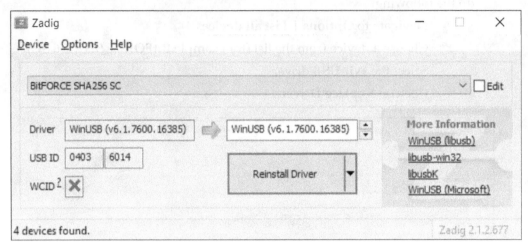

Fig. 5.5: Zadig shows the correct driver

4. Unplug and replug the USB miner.

5. Run `cgminer -n` to check if the mining device is recognized by cgminer:

Fig. 5.6: Before and after the driver installation, cgminer sees the BitFORCE ASIC

Once you have downloaded and extracted the software and set up the drivers, it is time to test if everything is working. Try connecting to your favorite mining pool with cgminer and if everything is configured correctly, you should be mining away.

To be consistent, we will use `https://www.multipool.us` for demonstration purposes.

Let's start mining

To connect cgminer to a pool, you will need, as usual, the relevant information:

- The URL of your pool
- The port number of the pool server
- Your mining pool username
- Your worker's name
- Your worker's password

Once you have all this information, you will run cgminer with the following options:

```
cgminer --url <poolurl:port> --userpass <USERNAME.WORKER:PASSWORD>
```

We can also use the short option identification:

```
cgminer -o <poolurl:port> -O <USERNAME.WORKER:PASSWORD>
```

As a concrete example, we will connect to the multipool, as shown:

```
cgminer -o stratum+tcp://us-west.multipool.us:9999 -O bit.miner:x
```

The following is an example of mining in Linux using cgminer, with BFL
BitFORCE ASIC:

```
┌─────────────────────────────── Terminal ──────────────────────── ↑ _ □ x
 File  Edit  View  Search  Terminal  Help
 cgminer version 4.9.2 - Started: [2015-08-30 16:03:25]
 --------------------------------------------------------------------------
 (15s):53.49G (1m):46.12G (5m):17.54G (15m):6.639G (avg):53.06Gh/s
 A:2560  R:0  HW:4  WU:775.4/m
 Connected to us-west.multipool.us diff 256 with stratum as user 0xfffff.280x
 Block: 960fbdb6...  Diff:54.3G  Started: [16:03:25]  Best share: 6.85K
 --------------------------------------------------------------------------
 [U]SB management [P]ool management [S]ettings [D]isplay options [Q]uit
 0: BAS FTWVRJ1R: max 70C 0.98V             | 53.66G / 53.09Gh/s WU:775.4/m
 --------------------------------------------------------------------------
 [2015-08-30 16:03:25] Network diff set to 54.3G
 [2015-08-30 16:03:29] Accepted 722938c1 Diff 574/256 BAS 0
 [2015-08-30 16:03:29] Stratum from pool 0 requested work restart
 [2015-08-30 16:03:54] Accepted fbb028b9 Diff 260/256 BAS 0
 [2015-08-30 16:03:54] Accepted d348e57f Diff 310/256 BAS 0
 [2015-08-30 16:04:18] Accepted a50662a4 Diff 397/256 BAS 0
 [2015-08-30 16:04:33] Accepted 79c0e937 Diff 538/256 BAS 0
 [2015-08-30 16:04:39] Accepted 0990801c Diff 6.85K/256 BAS 0
 [2015-08-30 16:04:58] Accepted 56b80ab9 Diff 756/256 BAS 0
 [2015-08-30 16:05:12] Accepted e5a7b95b Diff 285/256 BAS 0
 [2015-08-30 16:05:17] Accepted 1c1169b8 Diff 2.33K/256 BAS 0
 [2015-08-30 16:05:27] Accepted ff3e4e82 Diff 257/256 BAS 0
```

The following is an example of mining in Windows using cgminer, with BFL
BitFORCE ASIC:

```
Command Prompt - cgminer  -o stratum+tcp://us-west.multipool.us:9999 -O 0xfffff.280x:x        —    □    ×

cgminer version 4.9.2 - Started: [2015-08-23 21:31:24]
------------------------------------------------------------------------
(5s):53.31G (1m):53.32G (5m):49.66G (15m):31.50G (avg):53.29Gh/s
A:11008  R:0  HW:26  WU:735.4/m
Connected to us-west.multipool.us diff 256 with stratum as user 0xfffff.280x
Block: 59f3fed9...  Diff:54.3G  Started: [21:39:11]  Best share: 36.6K
------------------------------------------------------------------------
[U]SB management [P]ool management [S]ettings [D]isplay options [Q]uit
0: BAS FTWVRJ1R: max 77C 0.98V          | 52.67G / 53.29Gh/s WU:735.4/m
------------------------------------------------------------------------
[2015-08-23 21:40:36] Accepted c64fad1e Diff 330/256 BAS 0
[2015-08-23 21:41:01] Accepted 8638947f Diff 488/256 BAS 0
[2015-08-23 21:41:41] Accepted 280336ea Diff 1.64K/256 BAS 0
[2015-08-23 21:41:54] Accepted c1790063 Diff 339/256 BAS 0
[2015-08-23 21:41:55] Accepted 9930478d Diff 428/256 BAS 0
[2015-08-23 21:42:05] Accepted ddbb6c02 Diff 296/256 BAS 0
[2015-08-23 21:42:22] Accepted a72ee5e3 Diff 392/256 BAS 0
[2015-08-23 21:42:58] Accepted f001745f Diff 273/256 BAS 0
[2015-08-23 21:42:59] Accepted 7c66d667 Diff 527/256 BAS 0
[2015-08-23 21:43:02] Accepted dcd07c3f Diff 297/256 BAS 0
[2015-08-23 21:43:08] Accepted 93d33807 Diff 443/256 BAS 0
[2015-08-23 21:43:47] Accepted deb85d2b Diff 294/256 BAS 0
[2015-08-23 21:44:00] Accepted 01ca73a7 Diff 36.6K/256 BAS 0
[2015-08-23 21:44:00] Accepted 44c97ff1 Diff 953/256 BAS 0
```

What happens when mining on a ASIC

As you might remember from *Chapter 1*, *Bitcoin Wallets and Mining Software*, mining is all about hashing a candidate block and seeing if the hash meets certain difficulty criteria. On a CPU, we could only run as many threads as we had cores to do our mining. On a GPU, we could run hundreds or thousands of threads, thereby speeding up our computations.

However, both the CPU and GPU are designed for multi-purpose, universal computing. This means that both are capable of executing any valid code; in computing terms this is called **Turing-completeness**. On the other hand, ASICs are designed with only one purpose in mind. They are really fast at doing that one thing, but they cannot do anything else. The advantage lies in being able to optimize the microprocessor for the task required. This is the reason that ASICs are hundreds, even thousands of times faster than even the best GPUs at performing hashing calculations. Our demo ASIC, which is over two years old—ancient by Bitcoin ASIC standards—is approximately 60 times faster than a really good GPU.

When mining with an ASIC, the mining software creates the necessary work and the ASIC hashes away to find a possible solution. The mining software monitors all this work to make sure a valid solution, when found, is reported to the pool (when pool mining) or to the wallet (when solo mining). Don't worry; we will talk about both solo and pool mining in detail in later chapters.

Pros and cons of ASIC mining

Mining with an ASIC has its advantages and disadvantages. Let's examine these in order to understand if and when it is appropriate to use ASICs to mine Bitcoin. As you might recall, mining started on CPUs and then it moved over to GPUs, then briefly to FPGAs, and finally to ASICs. These machines are perhaps the last stop in hardware used for mining.

Currently, there isn't anything on the horizon that will replace ASICs any time soon. Quantum computers could theoretically be a candidate but such machines either do not exist or simply are not available to be acquired.

Pros of ASIC mining

ASIC mining is the fourth (and perhaps the last) step in mining hardware evolution. Currently all the serious miners, including professional installations, use different types of ASICs to mine. They are the most energy efficient of all miners and of course, they are also the fastest hashing machines available. If you think of yourself as a serious miner, you should be running ASICs only to mine for bitcoins.

To summarize, mining bitcoins with ASICs has the following advantages:

- ASICs are the fastest mining machines
- ASICs are the most energy efficient per unit of hashing
- Professional and business mining operations all use ASICs

Cons of ASIC mining

Competition among miners is fierce. As of August 30, 2015, there are approximately 415000 tera-hashes of mining power deployed. ASIC hardware costs roughly around 280 USD per tera-hash. In order to earn a single bitcoin per day, we will need on average (see the following calculation).

Network hashing speed divided by the number of bitcoins minted in a day, which, by plugging in current numbers yields the following:

```
415,000 /(144*25) ~= 115 tera-hashes of mining speeding
```

Purchasing such mining power requires an outlay of approximately 30000 USD. If a bitcoin can be sold for 300 USD and we are earning one per day, this means that we will need 100 days of running our hardware just to pay for it. If we factor in electricity, roughly 80 KW per hour, at an assumed rate of 10 US cents per KWh, then we have additional costs of $8 per hour (or $192 per 24 hour period).

As you can see the costs can add up quickly and electricity is a big part of it. It is very important to set up your mining operation where electricity is cheap or perhaps even free.

Some miners ignore the costs and hope for a big appreciation of the price of bitcoin. We believe such appreciation is possible. However, it is not too wise to bet on that outcome, as it is not guaranteed.

To summarize, mining bitcoin with ASICs has the following disadvantages:

* Electricity cost
* Hardware costs
* Fierce competition with other miners

Best practices when mining with ASICs

Let us look into the recommended things do to when mining with ASICs. Mining is fun and it can also be profitable if several factors are taken into account.

Make sure that all your ASICs have adequate cooling; additional fans beyond what is provided by the manufacturer are always a good idea. Remove dust frequently as a build up of dust might have a detrimental effect on the cooling efficiency and therefore mining speed.

For your particular mining machine, look up all the optimization tweaks online to get all the hashing power that is possible out of the device. Due to the large variety of mining machines, we cannot provide all the possible tweaks in our book.

When setting up a mining operation for profit, keep in mind that electricity costs will be a large percentage of your overall costs; hence, seek a location with the lowest electricity rates. Think about cooling costs; perhaps it will be the most beneficial to mine somewhere where the climate is cooler.

When purchasing ASICs, make sure that you calculate the cost per hash and also electricity used per hash. In mining, electricity is the biggest cost after hardware and over time, electricity will exceed the cost of the hardware. Note that the hardware costs fall over time, so purchasing your equipment in stages rather than all at once may be desirable.

To summarize, keep in mind these factors when mining with ASICs:

- Adequate cooling
- Optimization
- Electricity costs
- Hardware cost per GH/s

Benchmarks of mining speeds with different ASICs

As we have mentioned earlier, the Bitcoin network hash rate is really high now. Mining, even with ASICs, does not guarantee profits. This is due to the fact that during the mining process you are competing with other miners to try to solve a block. If those other miners are running a larger percentage of the total mining power, you will be at a disadvantage, as they are more likely to solve a block.

To compare the mining speed of a few ASICs, look at the following table:

ASIC	Mining speed GH/s	Power used watts
AntMiner S2	1000	1100
AntMiner S4	2000	1400
AntMiner S5	1155	590
ASICMiner BE Prisma	1400	1100
BFL Monarch	700	490
Black Arrow Prospero X-3	2000	2000
CoinTera TerraMiner IV	1600	2100
HashCoins Apollo V3	1100	1000
HashCoins Zeus v3	4500	3000

ASIC	Mining speed GH/s	Power used watts
KnC Neptune	3000	2100
Spondooliestech SP10	1400	1250
Spondooliestech SP35	5500	3650

Table. 5.1: Comparison of mining speed of different ASICs

ASIC versus FPGA, GPU, and CPU mining

As you can see from a comparison between *Table 5.1* and *Tables 4.1, 3.1*, and *2.1*, ASICs hash much faster than any other hardware. The fastest in our list almost reaches up to 5500 GH/s. That is a significant improvement over the other hardware. This is due to the massively optimized nature of application-specific microprocessors.

Profitability of ASIC mining

In calculating your potential profit, keep in mind the following factors:

- The cost of your ASICs
- Electricity costs to run the hardware
- Cooling costs — ASICs generate a decent amount of heat
- Your percentage of the total network hashing power

To calculate the expected rewards from mining, we can do the following. First, calculate what percentage of total hashing power you command. To look up the network mining speed, execute the `getmininginfo` command in the console of the Bitcoin Core wallet. We will do our calculations with an ASIC that can hash at 1 TH/s.

If the Bitcoin network hashes at 400000 TH/s, then our proportion of the hashing power is as follows:

```
1 /  400 000 = 0.0000025 of the total mining power.
```

On average, a Bitcoin block is found every 10 minutes, so six per hour and 144 for a 24-hour period. The current reward per block is 25 BTC, therefore in a day we have *144*25 = 3600* BTC mined.

If we command a certain percentage of the mining power, then on average we should earn that proportion of newly minted bitcoins.

Multiplying our portion of hashing power by the number of bitcoins minted daily we arrive at the following:

```
0.0000025 * 3600 BTC = 0.009 BTC
```

As one can see, that is roughly $2.5 USD for a 24 hour period.

For up-to-date profitability you can look at `https://www.multipool.us/` that publishes the average profitability per gigahash of mining power.

Summary

In this chapter, we explored ASIC mining. We explained how to install the mining software and how to set up the appropriate drivers; cgminer was our software of choice. We set it up on both Linux and Windows operating systems. We also connected to a mining pool to make sure everything was working as planned.

We examined the advantages and disadvantages of mining with ASICs. It will serve any miner well to ponder them when deciding to start mining or when thinking about improving current mining operations. We touched upon the best practices that we recommend to be kept in mind.

We also investigated the profitability of mining, given current conditions. A simple way of calculating, on average, your earnings was also presented. We concluded that mining competition is fierce; therefore, any improvements you can make will serve you well.

In the next chapter, we will look at the details of solo and pool mining.

6
Solo Versus Pool Mining

In this chapter, we will compare solo mining and pool mining. In the early days of Bitcoin mining, all mining was done solo; it was only later that mining pools emerged where miners pooled their hashing power together to ensure smoother and more predictable earnings. Today, most of the individual mining is done in pools. Only large, professional mining operations mine solo. We will guide you through the process of making an informed decision on whether to mine solo or to join a pool. Furthermore, we will summarize what characteristics are desirable in a pool, so that your decision of which pool to join will be easier to make. We will also go through the details of setting up your mining software and wallets, for both pool and solo mining.

We will delve into the following topics:

- Solo mining setup
- Pool mining setup
- Pool mining discussion
- Comparison of pool mining versus solo mining
- 51% attack against the Bitcoin network

Solo mining

In this chapter, we are assuming that you have your hardware connected and configured. Take a look at the previous chapters if you need help with configuring your mining hardware. Here, we will concentrate more on setup and the factors that will affect your decision to mine all by yourself versus mining with a pool.

Solo mining is the process of mining where a miner performs all calculations by him/herself. Any blocks found are credited to the miner and all rewards are kept by the miner. In solo mining, the miner competes against all other miners, pools, and individuals to solve a block.

Mining solo can be thought of as mining in a pool where you are the only worker. Instead of connecting to a pool, you will connect to your wallet and the wallet will act as a pool. The wallet gives the mining software all the necessary details in the form of a candidate block in order to start hashing it away. Therefore, running a wallet known as a full node is required for solo mining.

 Full Node is a Bitcoin wallet that has a complete local copy of the entire block chain. For example, the Bitcoin Core wallet is a full node.

Setting up a wallet for solo mining

Setting up a wallet for solo mining is not too difficult. You need to set a username, a password, and a port on which your mining software will connect and communicate with the wallet. Communication between the mining software and the wallet is via **Remote Procedure Call (RPC)**.

RPC is a client/server protocol where a program can communicate with and request service from another program. The network topology is not needed to be known, and all that is required is an IP address and port number.

All the required information is kept in a file called `bitcoin.conf`. This file can be found in the following directories:

- Linux: `~/.bitcoin directory`
- Windows: `C:\Users\User\AppData\Roaming\Bitcoin`
- MAC: `~/Library/Application Support/Bitcoin/`

By default, the file is not included in the Bitcoin distribution, so you will have to create it. The `bitcoin.conf` is a configuration file that is used to specify parameters to the bitcoin wallet software, as it starts up. The minimum contents of the file are, as follows:

```
rpcuser = <anything_you_want>
rpcpassword=<choose a good password here>
rpcallowip = 127.0.0.1
rpcallowip = 192.168.0.*
rpcport=12055
daemon=1
server=1
```

Let's go over each entry to make sure that we understand it all:

- **rpcuser**: This is the username your mining software will use to identify itself to your bitcoin wallet. You can choose any username.
- **rpcpassword**: This is the password your mining software will use in conjunction with `rpcuser` to identify itself to your bitcoin wallet.
- **rpcallowip**: This is the IP address that is allowed to connect to the wallet. We always allow the local address `127.0.0.1`. We also allow any computer on our local network to connect, by allowing `192.168.0.*`. The star specifies any valid number (from 0 to 255). Please note that `192.168.*.*` is a common IP range for private networks, but there are others as well. Check your local router to see the IPs your private network is using. You can also specify an IP range using a CIDR mask: `192.168.0/24`.
- **rpcport**: This is the port that programs use to connect to the wallet. You can choose any port that is free.
- **daemon**: This allows the wallet to run in the background, as a daemon, and accept commands.
- **server**: This allows the wallet to accept command-line and JSON-RPC commands.

The following screenshot depicts a sample `bitcoin.conf` file:

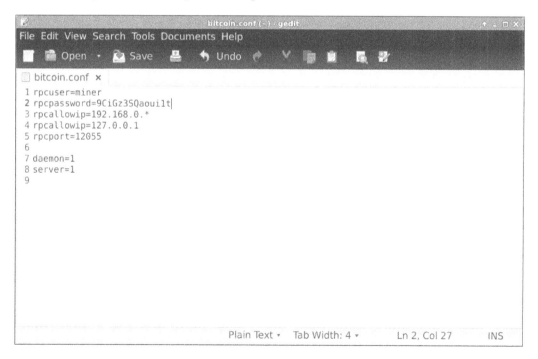

Setting up mining software for solo mining

There are many mining programs out there; our favorite is cgminer. We will refer to it here. In previous chapters, we showed you how to start cgminer with various options and parameters. (Note that for GPU mining you need to use cgminer version 3.7.2, while for mining with ASICs you should use the latest version.) When there are a lot of options and pools to specify, it gets tedious to type it all out, as a command.

To alleviate that inconvenience, cgminer allows the use of configuration files. We can put all the information in a file; when we start cgminer, we just point it to the file:

```
cgminer --config ~/.cgminer/solo.conf
```

In the preceding example, we reference a configuration file called `solo.conf` (shown in the following code). We will go over the details shortly. A cgminer configuration file is JSON-formatted. You can see a sample cgminer solo-mining configuration file in the following code snippet.

The following code is the sample configuration file:

```
{
"pools" : [
  {
    "url" : "127.0.0.1:12055",
    "user" : "username",
    "pass" : "password"
  }

],

"log" : "15"

}
```

In this code, we can see a sample solo-mining cgminer configuration file. We start off by specifying one or more pools. In case of solo mining, the pool is our wallet (IP `127.0.0.1` is the internal, loopback address of a computer). This is the case where the wallet and the mining software are on the same machine. We specify the IP, port, user name, and password so that cgminer is allowed to connect to the wallet. The user name and password are the same, as we have specified in the `bitcoin.conf` file.

After listing the details of our wallet, we are free to specify the additional options for cgminer. In our case, we only supplied the `-log` parameter, which specifies the interval in seconds between log outputs (`default: 5`).

Setting up mining software for pool mining

In the following screenshot, we can see a sample cgminer pool-mining configuration file. The file first specifies the number of pools.

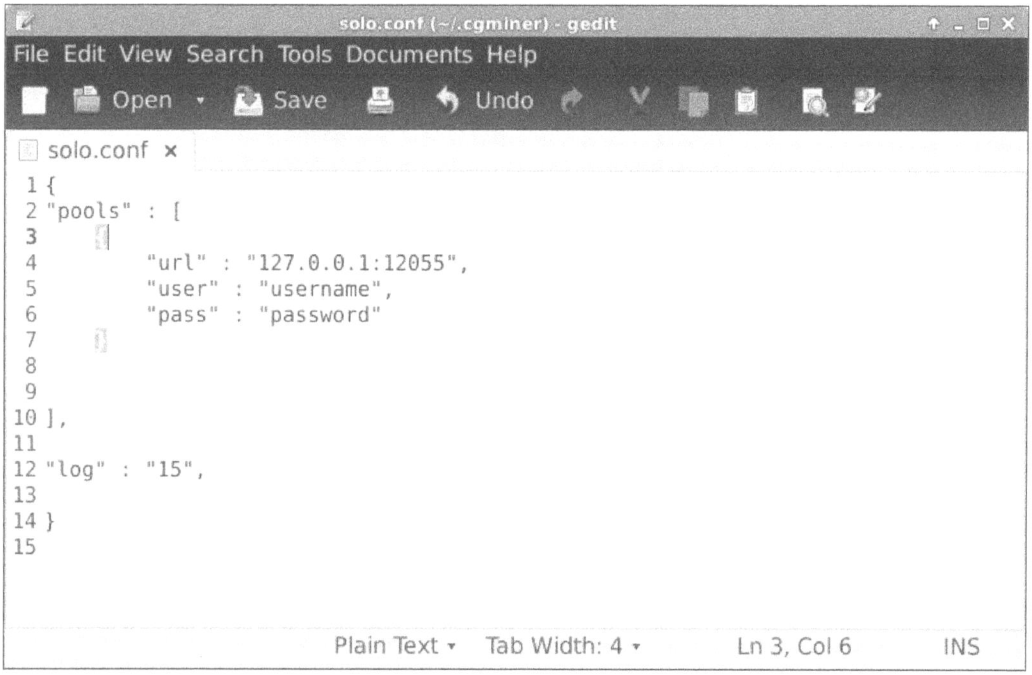

The following screenshot is the configuration file for multiple pools:

```
多                    multipool.conf (~/.cgminer) - gedit          ↑ _ □ ×

File  Edit  View  Search  Tools  Documents  Help

■  📂 Open  ▾   📄 Save    🖨    ↰ Undo    ↱   ∨   📋   📄   🔍   📝

▨ multipool.conf  ×

 1 {
 2 "pools" : [
 3      {
 4          "url" : "127.0.0.1:12055",
 5          "user" : "username",
 6          "pass" : "password"
 7      },
 8      {
 9          "url" : "stratum+tcp://us-west.multipool.us:9999",
10          "user" : "miner.bit",
11          "pass" : "x"
12      },
13      {
14          "url" : "stratum+tcp://pool2",
15          "user" : "miner.bit",
16          "pass" : "x"
17      },
18      {
19          "url" : "stratum+tcp://pool3",
20          "user" : "miner.bit",
21          "pass" : "x"
22      }
23
24
25 ],
26
27 "failover-only" : true,
28 "log" : "15",
29
30 }
31

                     Plain Text ▾   Tab Width: 4 ▾      Ln 4, Col 27      INS
```

The following code is the configuration file for multiple pools:

```
{
"pools" : [
  {
    "url" : "127.0.0.1:12055",
    "user" : "username",
    "pass" : "password"
```

```
      }

      {
        "url" : "stratum+tcp://us-west.multipool.us:9999",
        "user" : "miner.bit",
        "pass" : "x"
      },
      {
        "url" : "stratum+tcp://pool2",
        "user" : "miner.bit",
        "pass" : "x"
      },
      {
        "url" : "stratum+tcp://pool3",
        "user" : "miner.bit",
        "pass" : "x"
      }

   ],

   "failover-only" : true,
   "log" : "15"


}
```

You might be wondering why we have more than one pool listed; if our first pool of choice becomes unavailable or is temporarily down, cgminer will automatically switch to the next pool. This strategy is specified by the following option:

```
"failover-only" : true
```

 There are other strategies. We recommend consulting the README file that is included with cgminer. All the strategies are explained there in detail.

To connect cgminer to a pool you will need, as usual, the following relevant information:

- The URL of your pool
- The port number of the pool server
- Your mining pool user name
- Your worker's name
- Your worker's password

Let's go over the second pool entry in the file to see how the information is formatted:

```
{
    "url" : "stratum+tcp://us-west.multipool.us:9999",
    "user" : "miner.bit",
    "pass" : "x"
}
```

The information is self-explanatory, but for the sake of completeness, we specify it in the following code snippet:

```
{
    "url" : "url of the pool followed, by a colon followed, by the port
number",
    "user" : "your pool user name, followed by a period, followed by the
pool worker name",
    "pass" : "your pool worker's password specified on your pool, this
is usually just 'x' "
}
```

In order to use a configuration file with cgminer, we start cgminer with the `--config` parameter and point it to the location of the file. In our case:

```
cgminer --config ~/.cgminer/multipool.conf
```

If cgminer reads in the file successfully, that is the file has no errors, it will proceed to connect to our first pool and start hashing away. Since the file is in JSON format, you can check the syntax of the file at one of the many JSON syntax checkers online. This is the easiest way to find an error, in case there is one. There are also many ready configuration files posted online for different types of hardware. A quick search can save plenty of time.

Pool mining discussion

Pool mining started to appear in 2010. When you compete against other miners as a solo miner, your proportion of network hashing power may be small. As a result, you may only solve a block perhaps once a month or even once a year (depending on your hashing power). We can only calculate what the expected time to solve a block will be; however, we cannot predict exactly when it will happen.

To smooth out this variance, miners started to organize themselves into pools. In pool mining, a large number of miners work together to solve a block. Once someone in the pool finds a block, the rewards are shared among all miners belonging to the pool. This makes the payout more frequent, albeit smaller, and more predictable.

Mining pools

There is a variety of mining pools, with a variety of strategies. Perhaps the most popular (and fair) is the proportional pool. Here the reward is distributed to miners based on how much work they have contributed. How is a contribution calculated? As you recall, solving a block means finding a hash that falls below a certain threshold. The hash starts with a number of zeros; the higher the difficulty, the smaller the number representing the hash, and therefore the number of leading zeros is higher.

Miners working with a pool submit almost-solved-blocks, which are hashes of candidate blocks that aren't the difficulty required but some other, lower difficulty. This way the pool operator knows that the miner is in fact working on the block, as promised. These almost-solved-blocks are usually called shares, in pool lingo. In a proportional pool miners get paid proportionally, based on the number of shares they have found.

The most comprehensive comparison of mining pools can be found at `https://en.bitcoin.it/wiki/Comparison_of_mining_pools`. To see the current market share of the different pools, we recommend taking a look at `https://blockchain.info/pools`.

You can find the percentage market share of the most popular pools, as well as the number of blocks found in the specified time period. You can also click on the pool operator and see the blocks they have found. In turn, you can explore each block to see the transactions and other information. `https://blockchain.info/` is one of the so called block explorer websites. There are others, such as `https://blockexplorer.com`, `https://www.biteasy.com`, and `http://blockinfo.org`.

The following screenshot depicts the market share of the most popular bitcoin mining pools (over a period of four days):

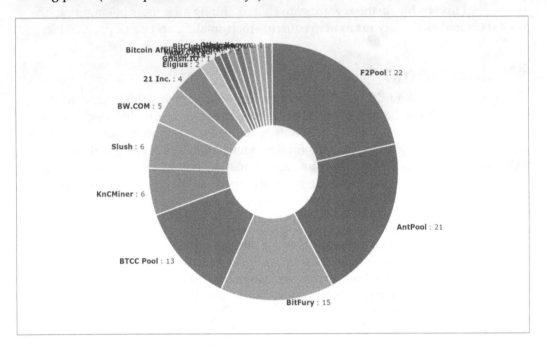

Choosing a pool

When you are choosing a pool, we recommend that you keep certain things in mind:

- First, understand that it is the pool operator that will be getting the block reward and then distributing it among the pool workers. Therefore, it is important to choose a reputable pool; a pool that has been in existence for a little while and has no incidents of misbehaving.

- Secondly, a pool that is geographically close to you will probably make sense, as the network latency will be minimal that way. Finally, joining one of the bigger pools, with more than 5% market share, may also be advantageous, as the payouts will be more frequent; although, they will be smaller.

Solo versus pool mining

There are a few things to consider when deciding whether to join a pool or mine alone. When it comes to bitcoin, unless you command at least 0.1% of the network hashing power (80 TH/s as of Jan 2016), we recommend joining a reputable pool. The reason is the variance in the frequency of solving blocks. With a small percentage of hashing power, finding blocks will be difficult; on average it will take a long time. Joining a pool, on the other hand, will make the payouts steadier and more predictable.

Profitability

Having 0.1% of the network hashing power means that on average one in 1000 blocks will be yours, which means roughly one per week.

In order to acquire 80 TH/s of ASIC hardware:

- You would have to invest roughly $36,000 USD at today's prices ($450 per TH)
- The ASICs would draw about 10000W of electricity (roughly $1 per hour, $24 per day; depending on, of course, where you are located)

If we can solve four blocks in a month, our revenue will be *100 BTC * $450 US = $45,000*. The electricity cost will be *$24 *30 = $720*.

It looks like we can make a profit of *$45,000 - $36,000 - $720 = $8280*. This is, of course, assuming that the network hashing power stays constant, the difficulty stays constant, and the bitcoin exchange rate doesn't decline. We cannot control these factors, and therefore it is nearly impossible to calculate a profit with any certainty.

Majority attack on Bitcoin

The design of Bitcoin allows for one obvious attack. The attack is called a 51% attack, after the amount of hashing power that is required to mount such an attack. At various times, mining pools have come close or have achieved 51% of the hashing power. A dishonest pool operator could use that hashing power to mount an attack. Therefore, a responsible miner should monitor the pool and when a pool gets close to that threshold, the miner should switch to another pool. Keeping the hashing power distributed is in everyone's interest.

51% attack

Let's now discuss what a 51% attacker can and cannot do. We'll start with what they cannot:

- An attacker cannot steal coins belonging to an existing address. This is because the attacker does not know the private key required to sign a transaction allowing transfer of the coins.

- The attacker, also, cannot prevent transactions from being propagated throughout the network, since we are assuming that the attacker does not control the network itself, only a majority of the hashing power.

- The attacker cannot change the block reward, as the rest of the network will not recognize the blocks with a different reward as valid. All the honest nodes will not accept blocks with a changed reward, and the attacker has no way to spend his bitcoins.

Any of the previously described attacks make no sense financially, as the amount to purchase or rent 51% of the hashing power will outweigh any financial benefits.

What an attacker can do is undermine confidence in Bitcoin. This would be possible if some powerful entity wanted to destroy Bitcoin. If the network found itself under attack, it would cause some to lose confidence in Bitcoin.

On the other hand, when an attack is discovered, developers work hard to fix it and honest nodes will probably implement the changes right away to try to save the network.

Summary

In this chapter, we explored solo mining and pool mining in more detail. We showed you how to set up your wallet and your mining software to be able to mine solo. We talked about the use of configuration files for the wallet and also configuration files for cgminer. We discussed mining pools and what to look for when joining one. We touched upon a very important attack against the network that every miner should be aware of—a 51% attack. In the next chapter, we will look at large-scale mining operations.

7

Large Scale Mining

In this chapter, we will examine **Large Scale Mining** (**LSM**). Bitcoin offers miners substantial rewards; as a result mining has emerged as a business. Some of these operations are well financed and are trying to achieve scale in order to realize the savings that come with it. They employ hundreds of tera-hashes of mining power. The biggest of these commercial mining operations have several peta-hashes of mining power. The Bitcoin network hashing speed recently reached one exa-hash. Mining at such a large scale has its own unique challenges. These large mining players are usually secretive to protect any advantages that they might have discovered; therefore, information about them is sparse. We will look into their operations, sometimes relying on facts and sometimes having to speculate, if the information is not available. LSM is an exciting era in Bitcoin mining and we hope that you will find it as interesting as we do.

We will delve into the following topics:

- Large Scale Mining overview
- LSM operations
- LSM challenges

Large Scale Mining overview

Bitcoin mining can be a profitable endeavor. Currently, the reward for finding a block is 25 BTC or about 10,000 US dollars at today's market price (Jan 2016). This reward is dispensed every 10 minutes on average. Financial reward is the main reason behind the emergence of Bitcoin mining on an industrial scale. In the last 2-3 years, a few entities have entered into the business of large-scale mining. The miners attempt to gain economies of scale, trying to find the sweet spot where costs are minimized to the optimum level.

Industrial miners face almost the same issues as data centers: access to relatively cheap power, good network access, access to latest hardware, and stable political climate. Then there are the demands of installing a lot of computing hardware inside a building: cooling, monitoring, and maintenance. To make things more difficult, miners get paid in bitcoins but their costs are in fiat currencies (Dollars, Euros, Kronas, and so on).

Definition

Fiat currency: This is the money that has been declared by a government to be the legal tender of a given country. Fiat money is not backed by any commodity or physical good. Usually, the material that it is made out of is worth much less than the face value printed on the note or coin.

Therefore, the exchange rate between bitcoin and fiat currency also affects the mining operations. In fact, the demands placed on miners are even more onerous than those on data center operators.

Bitcoin hardware becomes obsolete much faster than general purpose computing hardware. The most efficient operators sell their hardware just after a few months of usage. Some even get into manufacturing the equipment themselves to cut down on any delay in getting the latest hardware and deploying it as fast as possible. In the future, it is entirely possible that a majority of the network's hashing power will be owned by large, industrial-sized mines. Of course, the opposite is also possible. Imagine a mining chip embedded in all kinds of devices. By itself the chip may not have a lot of hashing power but hundreds of millions of them together will sum up to a significant amount of hashing power.

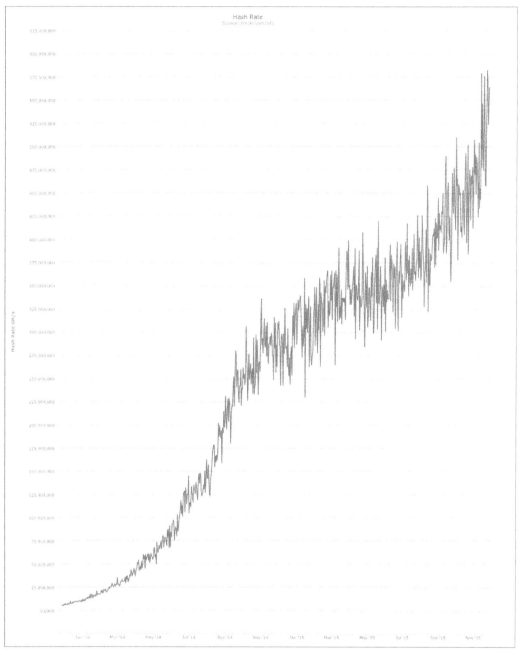

Fig. 7.1: The growth of the Bitcoin network hashrate. Mining is ultra competitive; in the last two years, the hashrate has increased almost 100-fold. Image courtesy of `https://blockchain.info/charts/hash-rate`

Large Scale Mining challenges

In addition to facing the same challenges as data centers, such as network connectivity, availability of electricity, and price, the largescale Bitcoin mines face numerous unique issues. The hardware replacement cycles are much shorter, measured in months rather than in years. The Bitcoin exchange rate is an external factor affecting the profitability, and the competition between the miners is fierce. Industrial Bitcoin miners were also the first to employ immersion cooling of components at a large scale. Let's examine the challenges in a little more detail.

Inexpensive and reliable electricity

One of the biggest costs for Bitcoin miners is the cost of electricity. Electricity is needed in both running the hardware and the associated cooling systems, be it fans or air conditioning. Miners, therefore, seek out locations where electricity is fairly priced. In order to save on cooling costs, they also seek locations with cooler climates. Iceland is a popular location for its abundance of power and for its cool climate. The Scandinavian countries are in demand because the arctic winds do a lot to cool the equipment. In North America, the biggest industrial Bitcoin mine is located in eastern Washington state due to the abundance of inexpensive hydroelectric power.

Good network connectivity

When a miner finds a block, it is really important to get it out to as many peers as possible. In case some other miner finds a block at the same time, you would want your block to be heard about first. Other miners will usually mine on top of the first block they hear about and so if they mine on top of yours, it is likely that your block will make it into the official blockchain and you will collect the coinbase reward. In order to give you an advantage in that regard, good network connectivity is a must; being connected to as many peers as the hardware allows is also a good idea.

Access to latest hardware

Mining is a competition against other miners. The more hashing power you command, the more likely you are to find the next block. Industrial Bitcoin mines update their equipment very often. Some locate themselves in close proximity to the hardware manufacturers, in order to minimize the cost of delivery and the time it takes to obtain and deploy the latest ASICs. Some equipment manufacturers even get into the mining game themselves. **KnC Miner** and **BitFury** are examples of ASIC manufacturers who mine with their own hardware and now command respectable hashing power. There have been mergers between mine operators and ASIC manufacturers to minimize costs and maximize efficiencies.

Stable political climate

It can cost up to millions of dollars to build a commercial mine. It is, therefore, a good idea to locate it in a jurisdiction that is either friendly to Bitcoin, or at least not against it. There are some mines in China, although the regulatory environment is not quite clear toward Bitcoin. Miners do prefer to set up operations where they can be confident to operate for quite some time without the fear of being banned. Currently, North America and most of Europe have a positive attitude toward Bitcoin. Consider the newest mine that BitFury is planning; it will be located in British Columbia, Canada.

Bitcoin exchange rate

As discussed earlier, miners' costs such as hardware, electricity, and staff are usually denominated in fiat currency, but their revenue is in bitcoins. As a result, the exchange rate between BTC and fiat is really important to miners, and it can have a big effect on operations. BTC peaked in Dec 2013, at approximately $1200 US. At that rate, 25 BTC translated to $30,000 US. Currently, the exchange rate is about $400 US, which yields a block reward of $10000 US. This is quite a big variance. The exchange rate fluctuation does present a challenge to industrial miners.

Another factor with respect to revenue is the halving of the block reward. As we remember, the reward for finding a Bitcoin block halves every 210,000 blocks or approximately every 4 years. The next expected halving will be in July 2016. The reward will decrease from today's 25 BTC to 12.5 BTC. Such a decrease in revenue will surely have some kind of an impact on miners. Luckily, the schedule of reward decreases is known in advance and therefore it gives time to the miners to prepare accordingly.

Outside resource

Track the reward halving at: http://www.bitcoinblockhalf.com/

Cooling of mining hardware

Bitcoin mining ASICs generate a lot of heat. As a result, the heat must be moved away from the machines, otherwise the machines might get overheated. When an ASIC overheats, it slows itself down to prevent damage. If that happens, efficiency suffers. Miners invest a sizable amount of capital in air conditioning systems, air movement systems (fans), liquid cooling systems, and recently into submersion cooling.

Immersion cooling is the next step in industrial Bitcoin mine cooling. All the mining chips are submersed in a cooling liquid that circulates to dissipate heat. Immersion cooling allows packing more chips per square foot in an industrial mine. The boards with the ASIC chips can be very close together. Furthermore, fans and heat sinks are no longer required. The ability to pack more processing power in a physical space is very important to a potential mine operator; lease agreements on warehouses are usually priced on a per square foot basis.

Allied Control has built an immersion-cooled mine in Hong Kong in 2013. It is a 500-kW installation taking up only 300 square feet of space.

Prediction

Future space heaters can be built around ASICs. Imagine an ASIC miner that acts as a heater; it will then serve a dual purpose: heating and securing the Bitcoin network.

Large Scale Mining operations

We can look at block explorers to see which entities are finding the most blocks. Those entities are either big mining pools or industrial Bitcoin mines. We took a look at `https://blockchain.info/pools` to see the hashrate distribution, which is depicted in the following figures:

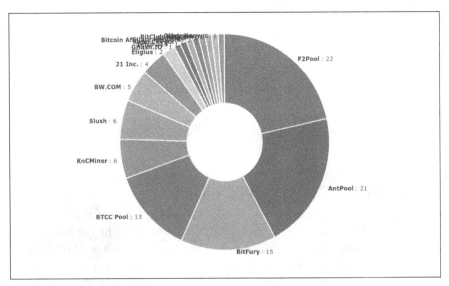

Fig. 7.2: Hashrate distribution (4-day average). Image courtesy of `blockchain.info` (you can take a look at `https://blockchain.info/pools` or `https://www.smartbit.com.au/` to see the latest distribution)

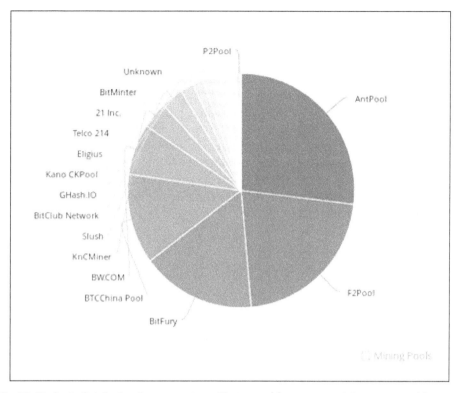

Fig. 7.3: Hashrate distribution. Image courtesy of https://www.smartbit.com.au/ (you can take a look at https://blockchain.info/pools or https://www.smartbit.com.au/ to see the latest distribution)

We can see that the two biggest holders of hashrates are **F2Pool** and **AntPool**; those are the mining pools. So are **BTCChina Pool**, **Slush**, **BW.COM**, **Eligius**, **BitMinter**, and **GHash.IO**.

On the other hand, **BitFury**, **KnC Miner**, **21Inc.**, and **Telco 214** are industrial miners ranging from very large to small. Let's see what is known about these companies.

BitFury

BitFury is the largest industrial miner in the Bitcoin ecosystem. Currently, it holds about 15% of the total network hashing power, roughly 75-80 peta-hashes. Its mining operations are located in Iceland and Georgia. The company is very well funded, often earning the title of the best-funded miner in Bitcoin. BitFury is moving to a 16nm (1nm, nanometer = one billionth of a meter) chip, but it is not clear whether the company has already deployed it or not. In September 2015, BitFury announced plans to build a 100 MW mining facility in the Republic of Georgia. It has been reported that this facility will be using immersion cooling. Immersion cooling in the Bitcoin space was pioneered by **Allied Control**, a company that BitFury recently acquired. Immersion cooling is the best possible way to cool electronics as of today and probably far into the future.

Outside resource
BitFury website: http://www.bitfury.org/

KnC Miner

KnC Miner is a Swedish company engaged in the manufacturing of ASIC chips. The company is well funded, having raised multimillion dollar rounds of financing. The company used to sell its ASIC miners to consumers, but it has now discontinued those operations in order to concentrate on running its hardware to mine for bitcoin and to secure the blockchain. Its mines are located in the Arctic Circle, benefiting from the cool climate and from the locally-sourced, cheap hydroelectric power. In 2015, KnC Miner opened a new mine located in an 18,000 square-foot warehouse. Not much information has been released about that operation, other than the fact that it will deploy the newest KnC chips. Currently KnC, just like Bitfury, has moved to a 16nm design; the company claims that the new chip is six times faster than the previous 28nm design. In November 2015, KnC held about 6% of the hashrate, which will put it around 32 peta-hashes.

KnC's earlier industrial mine was a 13 MW facility on 156,000 sq ft. That mine is most likely not in operation at the moment, unless the hardware was upgraded. The facility employed a staff of 30 to keep everything running smoothly. The cooling method in that installation was assumed to be free-air-cooling, as in using the cold Arctic wind to cool the chips. This is, however, only a speculation, as KnC does not provide too much information about their mine operations.

Outside resource
KnC website: http://www.kncminer.com/

21 INC

21 INC is a relatively new company. Its mission is to build the hardware infrastructure that the Bitcoin ecosystem will require to realize its full potential. Their plan is to put Bitcoin mining in a large variety of small devices. To that end, 21 INC has already released its "first Bitcoin computer". It is a small factor computer (think the size of a smartphone) with a built-in mining chip. It seems that all the 21 INC computers mine on a pool set up by 21 INC. Currently, 21 INC has 4% of the total mining power, which translates to about 22 peta-hashes. 21 INC seems like an innovative company and we are curious about what it will do in the near to long term future.

Outside resource
21 INC website: `https://21.co/`

Mega Big Power

Perhaps the most publicized bitcoin mine is the Mega Big Power mine located in eastern Washington state, in the USA. The exact location is not known, but it is assumed that it was located close to a hydroelectric generation facility for its cheap power. Mega Big Power allowed reporters into its facility to tour and view it. There are even YouTube videos showcasing the mine. In mid-2014, the mine had an impressive 1 peta-hash of mining power. It is not clear whether the mine is still in operation and if it was upgraded to new equipment. According to their website, it seems that the company has moved into the business of running mines for other people. They have created what they call a franchisee program.

Outside resources
Mega Big Power Bitcoin mine videos: `https://www.youtube.com/watch?v=-ihMqEDs4B8`
Mega Big Power website: `https://megabigpower.com`

Genesis Mining

Genesis Mining is a company that offers cloud-based mining contracts. They sell mining hash power to anyone who is willing to pay for it. Basically, the company runs its own mine but rents out the hardware on a per-computing power basis to third parties. Whether cloud mining is profitable or not for the buyer of the contract is not our focus here. If you do decide to purchase such contracts, make sure to research them well. We have mentioned Genesis Mining here because they have a couple of videos on their website that are worth taking a look at. They also provide a live camera feed at their facility in Iceland. Another noteworthy development from Genesis is their Hive software to monitor and maintain large mining installations. Genesis claims that the software is the first of its kind. It currently advertises the software for sale to interested parties.

Outside resources

Genesis Mining website: https://www.genesis-mining.com/

Live camera feed: http://www.lifeinsideabitcoinmine.com/

Genesis Hive: https://genesis-hive.com/

Other mine operators

The preceding list is by no means exhaustive. Rather, it was meant to be an example of the industrial-scale miners out there. The Bitcoin mining space also evolves very rapidly and things change fast. In a year or two, the landscape of large-scale miners may look completely different.

There are no doubt other mine operators in existence that simply choose to remain in stealth mode. It is possible for a large mine to contribute hashing power to several pools and therefore not be noticed.

Summary

In this chapter, we explored LSM operations. We defined what it means to run a large scale mining operation. We presented and explained the challenges that such operations face today. Most likely, these challenges will evolve, some will become non-issues, and others will become dominant. We also looked into the operations of some of the most well-known miners who run industrial-sized mines. The field of large scale mining is relatively new and we expect lots of developments and perhaps the emergence of completely new players in the game. It is an exciting time to be watching and commentating on Bitcoin mining.

In the next chapter, we will look at what the future of mining may look like. We will examine the centralization of mining debate and consider if there is a chance that mining can become more decentralized than it is today.

8
The Future of Bitcoin Mining

In this chapter, we will speculate about the future of Bitcoin mining. This is rather a fun chapter, as we can't be absolutely certain about what will happen. We can however, make educated guesses about where things may be headed. We will explore the possible ways in which mining may either become very centralized or go the opposite way and become decentralized.

There has also been a concern that mining pools have become too big. However, we think those concerns are not justified. After Ghash.IO became, for a brief moment, the biggest pool with more than 50% of mining power, miners moved their rigs to other pools and Ghash withered to about 3% of the network hashing capacity.

The following topics will be covered in this chapter:

- Further centralization of mining power
- Decentralization of mining and mining chips in all kinds of devices
- Eliminating **Proof of Work (PoW)** in favor of something else
- Can we do without mining?

Overview of the current state of mining

As of early 2016, mining is on its way to become more centralized. Mining equipment manufacturers are increasingly mining for themselves and not selling the hardware to consumers. Some of the bigger manufacturers now command 15% or more of the network's total hashing power. Recently, there has been a big run up of the hashing power. In the span of about a month, the hashrate jumped from 500 to 750 peta-hashes. In January 2016 it reached one exahash, and currently (Feb 2016) it is around 1.3 exahashes. (see `https://blockchain.info/charts/hash-rate` for up to date information).

Further centralization of mining

It is quite possible that mining may become more centralized. In the summer of 2016, the block reward will halve to 12.5 BTC; this development may move some of the smaller miners into an unprofitable territory; hence, forcing them to stop mining. As a result, the big miners may end up with a bigger overall percentage of the hashrate. Manufacturers of mining equipment constantly put out better, faster, and more efficient hardware. There is a consolidation happening in this space; thereby, creating larger mining entities. Quantum computing may also introduce a miner with enormous hash-power, and of course, if the BTC value, as measured against local currency, skyrockets, then it will encourage more investment into mining equipment from large established mining firms.

Hardware arms race

In order to mine profitably, your hardware needs to be better than that of your competitors. Currently, Bitcoin mining ASIC manufacturers are in a kind of hardware arms race, trying to bring newer and more efficient ASICs online faster than anyone else. This race cannot continue forever. There are physical limits to chip design, and past a certain point there will be little or no room left for improvement. However, for now, these manufacturers are competing fiercely with one another and thereby gaining a bigger share of the mining rewards pie.

Halving of the reward

The next halving of the block reward may result in some miners taking their hardware offline. Their fixed costs will still be the same, but their revenue will be cut in half. Unless the exchange rate of BTC to fiat doubles to ensure that miners' revenue in fiat currency stays the same as before, some mining equipment will have to be disconnected. If such a scenario presents itself, then the bigger miners will be left with a larger percentage of the total hashrate.

Outside resource

See the reward schedule at `https://en.bitcoin.it/wiki/Controlled_supply`

Consolidation, mergers, and acquisitions

The competition between miners is fierce. Every miner is racing to find a solution to the current block before another miner. Competition like this in any other sector leads to strategic alliances. We already saw Spondoolies, an ASIC hardware manufacturer, merge with BTCS. BitFury acquired Allied Control, the immersion cooling specialist. It is to be expected that more transactions similar to these will take place. Will we see one mining entity get to the 50% threshold? We doubt it, but we cannot ignore that possibility.

Bitcoin exchange rate

Miners earn their revenue in bitcoins, but usually their costs are in local currency. If the value of bitcoin versus fiat currency skyrockets, we might see big mining outfits throw even more hardware at the Bitcoin blockchain. The miners' revenue will soar in local currency and mining will be more profitable; so it is understandable that further investment in mining hardware might occur.

Outside resource

You can view the exchange rate at http://winkdex.com/

Quantum computing and mining

This is quite a long shot; however, if quantum computing becomes a reality, some entity may decide to use it for mining. If a quantum computer performs as expected, there might be the possibility that a lot of hashing power may suddenly be controlled by the entity that decided to deploy quantum computers for mining.

Outside resource

More quantum computing information: https://en.wikipedia.org/wiki/Quantum_computing

Cracking the security of SHA-256

Some observers say that it is possible that at some point of time the hash function used in mining could be cracked by somebody. If that happens, the entity that cracked it will be able to solve all the blocks before anyone else. Of course, to continue minting blocks, they should not solve all of them as it would become known that they have some kind of an unfair advantage.

> **Prediction**
> It is our opinion that the SHA-256 hash function will be replaced by a more secure function within a decade.

Centralization by region

A concentration of mining power in certain regions might give rise to theories of governmental pressure on miners and therefore an indirect governmental control of the Bitcoin network. A large percentage of mining power is currently located in China; it is plausible that when necessary, the Chinese government can perhaps require miners to censor the blockchain by excluding transactions and blacklisting transactions. In our opinion, such pressure will drive miners to other jurisdictions, but it is difficult to predict the behavior of miners. We assume that miners only mine for economic gain and no other reasons. If the cheapest electricity is found in China, then perhaps the demands of the government can be overlooked. We are mentioning this here as it is something that is interesting to watch, as it unfolds.

Governments adopting cryptocurrencies

There has been some speculation about governments adopting digital currencies. This is a good idea, but it is uncertain if central banks would support such a move. A proposal called **Fedcoin** has been circulating around the web for quite some time. It suggests that the Federal Reserve creates a blockchain-based currency called **Fedcoin**. Fedcoin will be a digital dollar backed by the Fed and therefore its value will always be 1 dollar. The first government with a solid currency to issue a digital version of their currency might witness their currency being used worldwide quite quickly. A digital dollar will be a favorite in developing nations where inflation is high.

We might also see a government adopting Bitcoin as an official currency, although we doubt that it will happen, as monetary policy will be taken away from the central bank of that nation. Perhaps, Bitcoin can be adopted by a nation as an addition to their fiat currency and not as a replacement of it.

Decentralization of mining

It is quite possible that mining power will become more decentralized as opposed to more consolidated. Mining chips might be embedded in a variety of devices, from fridges, cars, and light bulbs to any device that creates heat. If that were to occur, a large portion of the network hash power could be made up by the millions of tiny mining chips embedded everywhere.

Mining chips everywhere

A possible scenario that may develop is, mining chips being included in all kinds of devices. We can see that any electronic device or household appliance can have a mining chip included. The Internet of Things can also speed up the inclusion of mining chips everywhere. The "Things" on the Internet of Things can be earning and spending satoshis on a variety of services or products. It is quite possible that every one of us could become a Bitcoin miner, if mining chips become ubiquitous.

21 INC and the Bitcoin Computer

The first example of an embedded mining chip is most likely the Bitcoin Computer from 21 INC. If their plan of selling millions of them pans out, there will be a lot of mining chips out there. Together, those chips will add up to significant computing power. 21 INC already has 3% of the network hashing power, only a few months after releasing their device.

Mining devices as a source of heat

Mining chips generate heat while hashing; as a result, they can be used in a variety of things that generate heat. Heaters can mine and distribute the heat that the chips create. Electric blankets can also be constructed with mining ASICs. There is even a possibility for light bulbs to mine as well. Heating in electric cars can also utilize mining chips. Such heating devices will cost more than ordinary heaters, but they will have the potential to pay for themselves over their lifetime.

The end of the ASIC arms race is near

Currently ASIC manufacturers are locked in a race to deliver more and more efficient mining chips. That race could soon reach a point where there is very little or no room for improvement. The manufacturing process is now down to 11nm (1 nm, or nanometer is one billionth of a meter), and it's doubtful if chip manufacturing can improve much more beyond this point. This will allow further decentralization as hardware will not depreciate and become obsolete as fast as it did in the past. If depreciation slows, individual miners may return to Bitcoin mining, as the hardware would pay for itself over time.

Decentralized mining is key

Bitcoin's reputation as a decentralized system depends upon keeping the mining fairly decentralized. Although it is highly unlikely that a miner will act maliciously in the event of obtaining the majority of the network hash power. However, it is better for everyone involved that no single miner reaches this threshold. A decentralized mining system gives a lot of participants in the Bitcoin experiment peace of mind. After all, there is some serious money at stake now. Bitcoin's market cap, as of early 2016, is around 7 billion US dollars.

Elimination of PoW

Proof of work may not be the best algorithm to secure a blockchain-based system. There are aspects of PoW that leave a lot to be desired. However, PoW is a good way to distribute a digital currency. Perhaps PoW will be replaced in the future by something different, but at this time we cannot say for certain what it will be.

Inefficiency of PoW

Proof of Work is really inefficient; it wastes a lot of electricity and computing power. However, it is inefficient by design. We do want competition between miners because that is precisely what makes the blockchain ledger secure. Miners keep other miners honest because they are all competing for the same block reward. We believe that PoW is the best way to distribute a cryptocurrency, initially. Perhaps after bitcoins are fully, or almost fully, distributed, it will make sense to switch to another algorithm to secure the blockchain.

Replacement of PoW

Currently, we are not sure what should be used instead of PoW. There are candidates, such as Proof of Stake, in which the right to mint a block depends on the amount of currency that the miner holds. Of course, that scheme is not perfect either and has its own unique drawbacks. For example, it encourages hoarding of currency. Another possibility is to repurpose the current PoW algorithm to do something useful. The cryptocurrency Primecoin uses proof of work to find special chains of primes, known as **Cunningham chains** and **bi-twin chains**. Cunningham chains as well as bi-twin chains are sequences of prime numbers that meet certain criteria; if you are interested in these, take a look at the following links. They are interesting if you are a fan of number theory, but they are not related to Bitcoin mining at all.

Outside resource:
https://en.wikipedia.org/wiki/Cunningham_chain
https://en.wikipedia.org/wiki/Bi-twin_chain

Perhaps a new and clever algorithm will be developed that can secure the Bitcoin blockchain in a way that is currently unimaginable; we have to allow for that possibility as well. As the number of bright minds attracted to the blockchain concept increases, then more and more research will be undertaken to improve all aspects of the technology including mining.

Can we do without mining?

Mining is the way by which we currently secure the Bitcoin blockchain and in conjunction with PoW it is used to distribute the newly minted bitcoins. But is mining, as we know it today, necessary? Can we do away with it and replace it with something better, something perhaps more efficient?

Replacing or eliminating mining

Theoretically, we can eliminate or replace mining with some other form of securing the blockchain. As discussed earlier, by replacing PoW with Proof of Stake we could eliminate mining, as we know it today. Of course, a secure blockchain is the number one concern, so we must be sure that switching to another algorithm will not compromise security. Therefore, mining as we know it today is technically not necessary, but it is the only secure way we know of today. There has not been enough research done regarding other algorithms to switch Bitcoin over to something else. Unless some amazing new way of securing the blockchain gets discovered soon, we do not foresee a change in Bitcoin mining for at least a decade or so.

Efficiency of mining

A lot of newcomers to Bitcoin complain about the inefficiency of Bitcoin mining. This is understandable, for years, computing science schools pushed efficiency onto their students. Efficiency is one of the most important goals in software design. In decentralized systems, however efficiency is secondary and redundancy becomes the number one concern. Bitcoin mining is inefficient on purpose. The competition between miners is what keeps them honest. One way is to view this as inefficient, another way is to view it as a price to pay for a decentralized system, where no single party has total control over the system. So when thinking about a replacement of mining, keeping efficiency in mind is a good idea, but realizing that the inefficiency serves a purpose is more important.

Possible ways in which mining may change

We do not foresee big changes happening to Bitcoin mining soon; it is a good mental exercise to think of ways in which mining could be changed. An obvious candidate for change is the much-debated PoW algorithm. Of course the SHA-256 hash function will be replaced sometime in the future by the next generation of hash functions. But what about the more fundamental changes? Perhaps Bitcoin mining will become so ubiquitous (mining chips everywhere) that we will just take it for granted. In our opinion, this is the most likely scenario in the event that blockchains become mainstream. Perhaps all blockchains will be mined together. Merged mining already exists, wherein miners submit their solutions to more than one blockchain.

Outside resources
Merged mining:
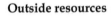
http://bitcoin.stackexchange.com/questions/273/how-does-merged-mining-work

https://en.bitcoin.it/wiki/Merged_mining_specification

We can also imagine more drastic changes. Perhaps, someone will figure out a way to go back to "one CPU one vote", as Satoshi originally envisioned. Although Bitcoin purists prefer that approach, it is not without its drawbacks. A hacker with a vast botnet could easily undermine the security of the underlying blockchain. It's also very likely that mining will contribute its resources to solve some kind of real-world problem (à la Primecoin). It is also possible that mining will be replaced by something that we cannot foresee today.

Summary

In this chapter, we explored what may be in store for Bitcoin Mining. Mining may become more centralized and there is evidence to support that argument. At the same time, it is also possible that mining will become more decentralized. We are already seeing steps being taken in that direction. PoW, while being a good algorithm for initial distribution of a digital currency, may not be the best way to secure the blockchain in the future. We will probably see PoW being replaced by a different algorithm.

We hope that you have enjoyed reading this book as much as we have enjoyed putting it together. Mining is an exciting topic to discuss and even more exciting to practice. We encourage you to put what you have learned in this book into practice by setting up a miner of your own. You can set up and configure the hardware and software required by following the instructions in previous chapters. You will gain some knowledge and you will be able to say that you were a part of Bitcoin mining.

We are great proponents of the blockchain technology and we believe that in the future blockchains will be the basis for many applications. A quick Internet search will reveal the enormous interest that blockchains currently command. There are a number of start-ups devoted to furthering this technology. Lately, even established businesses have been joining the blockchain bandwagon. We see the likes of major banks and large IT and software companies working on blockchain technology.

In its current implementation, blockchains require a healthy mining ecosystem to secure them. Without this security, blockchains lose their appeal. It is therefore vital to understand that miners perform a very important function that should not be underestimated. We hope that this book will give you some insight into the interesting world of blockchain mining in general, with the emphasis on cryptocurrency mining. It is quite likely that cryptocurrencies of all flavors will have a bright future. Bitcoin in particular is the clear leader in this field and we cannot see a scenario where some other currency overtakes it any time soon. Bitcoin is an evolving (albeit slowly) system that can incorporate the best ideas from cryptocurrencies that may challenge it.

Some observers compare Bitcoin and blockchains to the Internet in 1995, and we all know how far the Internet has gone in the last two decades. We encourage you to get involved with cryptocurrencies and blockchains right now, as they are still in their infancy and have not reached the mainstream yet. This is an exciting and interesting field that has the potential to truly change the world.

Index

Symbols

21 INC
about 95, 103
URL 95
/apps/cgminer
URL 39

A

ADL SDK library
URL 41
Allied Control 94
AMD APP SDK
URL 40
AMD drivers
URL 38
AntPool 93
ASIC manufacturers 103
ASIC mining
best practices 71, 72
cons 70, 71
defining 70
profitability 73, 74
pros 70
versus CPU mining 73
versus FPGA 73
versus GPU 73

B

Bitcoin
51% attack 85
defining 87
references 100
Bitcoin block halves
URL 91

Bitcoin Computer 103
Bitcoin Core
about 1
mining with 25-28
Bitcoin mining 16
Bitcoin wallet
defining 1, 2
need for 2, 3
Bitcoin, with ASICs
advantages 70
BitFury
about 90-93
URL 94
BitMinter 93
bi-twin chains
about 104
URL 104
block 2
block explorer
URL 83
BTCChina Pool 93
BW.COM 93

C

Central Processing Unit (CPU) 25
cgminer
installing, on Linux 52, 53
installing, on Windows 53, 54
references 62
setting up, for pool mining 79-82
setting up, for solo mining 78
URL 52
using 52
challenges, Large Scale Mining (LSM)
access, to latest hardware 90

Bitcoin exchange rate 91
cooling, of mining hardware 91, 92
good network connectivity 90
inexpensive and reliable electricity 90
stable political climate 91
chips
mining 103
client 2
CPUMiner
about 29
URL 29
CPU mining
versus FPGA and GPU mining 57
versus GPU mining 49
cryptocurrencies
adopting 102
URL 29
Cunningham chains
about 104
URL 104

D

decentralized mining 104
devices
mining 103

E

Eligius 93
exchange rate
URL 101

F

F2Pool 93
Fedcoin 102
Fiat currency 88
Field-Programmable Gate
Arrays (FPGAs) 51
FPGA mining
best practices 56
cons 56
mining speed, comparing 57
performing 55
profitability 58

pros 55
software requisites 51
starting 54
versus GPU and CPU mining 57
full clients 2
Full Node 76

G

Genesis Hive
URL 96
Genesis Mining website
URL 96
GHash.IO 93
GitHub repository
URL 39
GPU
drivers 37-39
mining 45
mining software 39, 40
mining speeds, defining 48
multiple GPU setup 44, 45
setting up, for mining 37
GPU mining
about 46
best practices 47
cons 46, 47
profitability 49
pros 46
versus CPU mining 49
versus FPGA and CPU mining 57

H

hardware wallets
about 12
advantages 13
hosted wallets 13

K

KnC Miner
about 94
URL 94

L

Large Scale Mining (LSM)
about 87
challenges 90
defining 87, 88
Ledger website
URL 13
Linux
cgminer, installing on 52, 53
Linux commands
cgminer -n 39
cgminer -V 39
defining 38, 39
lspci | grep VGA 38
sudo aticonfig --adapter=all --odgt 38
Live camera feed
URL 96

M

Mega Big Power Bitcoin mine videos
URL 95
Mega Big Power website
URL 95
merged mining
references 106
mining
about 31, 32, 67, 68
changes, implementing 106
cons 32
decentralization 102
defining 99, 100
efficiency 106
eliminating 105
need for 33, 105
on ASIC 69, 70
profitability 34, 35
pros 32
replacing 105
requisites 100-102
mining pools
about 83
reference link 83
URL 92

mining software
about 14, 29
cgminer, connecting to pool 42-44
cgminer, installing on Linux 62-64
cgminer, installing on Windows 64-67
defining 62
drivers 62
Linux installation instructions 40-42
need for 14
references 15
selecting 15-22
setting up 62
using 15
Windows installation instructions 40
mining speed
benchmarks, with different ASICs 72
comparing 48, 72
mining, with CPUs
best practices 33
multipool
about 29
URL 29

O

operations, Large Scale Mining (LSM)
21 INC 95
BitFury 94
defining 92, 93
Genesis Mining 96
KnC Miner 94
Mega Big Power 95
mine operators 96

P

pool mining
about 82
mining pools 83
mining software, setting up 79-82
pool, selecting 84
profitability 85
versus solo mining 85
pools
reference link, for market share 83

precompiled binaries
  URL 29
precompiled releases, for MAC
  URL 39
Proof of Work (PoW)
  about 99
  eliminating 104
  inefficiency 104
  replacing 104

Q

Quantum Computing
  URL 101

R

Remote Procedure Call (RPC) 76

S

satoshi 33
Simplified Payment Verification (SPV) 13
Slush 93
software requisites, FPGA mining
  cgminer 52
software wallets
  about 3-11
  references 3
solo mining
  about 75, 76
  mining software, setting up 78
  versus pool mining 85
  wallet, setting up 76, 77

T

Telco 214 93
thin wallets 1
Trezor website
  URL 13
Turing-completeness 55, 69

V

Video Cards 37

W

wallet
  setting up, for solo mining 76, 77
wallet security 14
wallet types
  about 3
  full wallet, versus thin client 13
  hardware wallets 12, 13
  hosted wallets 13
  software wallets 3-12
  wallet security 14
Windows
  cgminer, installing on 53, 54
Worksize
  URL 44

Z

zadig utility
  about 64
  URL 64

Thank you for buying
Bitcoin Essentials

About Packt Publishing

Packt, pronounced 'packed', published its first book, *Mastering phpMyAdmin for Effective MySQL Management*, in April 2004, and subsequently continued to specialize in publishing highly focused books on specific technologies and solutions.

Our books and publications share the experiences of your fellow IT professionals in adapting and customizing today's systems, applications, and frameworks. Our solution-based books give you the knowledge and power to customize the software and technologies you're using to get the job done. Packt books are more specific and less general than the IT books you have seen in the past. Our unique business model allows us to bring you more focused information, giving you more of what you need to know, and less of what you don't.

Packt is a modern yet unique publishing company that focuses on producing quality, cutting-edge books for communities of developers, administrators, and newbies alike. For more information, please visit our website at www.packtpub.com.

About Packt Open Source

In 2010, Packt launched two new brands, Packt Open Source and Packt Enterprise, in order to continue its focus on specialization. This book is part of the Packt Open Source brand, home to books published on software built around open source licenses, and offering information to anybody from advanced developers to budding web designers. The Open Source brand also runs Packt's Open Source Royalty Scheme, by which Packt gives a royalty to each open source project about whose software a book is sold.

Writing for Packt

We welcome all inquiries from people who are interested in authoring. Book proposals should be sent to author@packtpub.com. If your book idea is still at an early stage and you would like to discuss it first before writing a formal book proposal, then please contact us; one of our commissioning editors will get in touch with you.

We're not just looking for published authors; if you have strong technical skills but no writing experience, our experienced editors can help you develop a writing career, or simply get some additional reward for your expertise.

Kali Linux Wireless Penetration Testing Essentials

ISBN: 978-1-78528-085-6   Paperback: 164 pages

Plan and execute penetration tests on wireless networks with the Kali Linux distribution

1. Learn the fundamentals of wireless LAN security and penetration testing.

2. Discover and attack wireless networks using specialized Kali Linux tools.

3. A step-by-step, practical guide to wireless penetration testing with hands-on examples.

Raspberry Pi Server Essentials

ISBN: 978-1-78328-469-6   Paperback: 116 pages

Transform your Raspberry Pi into a server for hosting websites, games, or even your Bitcoin network

1. Unlock the various possibilities of using Raspberry Pi as a server.

2. Configure a media center for your home or sharing with friends.

3. Connect to the Bitcoin network and manage your wallet.

Please check **www.PacktPub.com** for information on our titles

www.ingramcontent.com/pod-product-compliance
Lightning Source LLC
Chambersburg PA
CBHW060153060326

40690CB00018B/4092